W9-AQT-338

# Paper-Pieced Mini Quilts

## WENDY VOSTERS

**Martingale®**
& COMPANY

Paper-Pieced Mini Quilts
© 2007 by Wendy Vosters

That Patchwork Place® is an imprint of Martingale & Company®.

Martingale & Company
20205 144th Ave. NE
Woodinville, WA 98072-8478
www.martingale-pub.com

No part of this product may be reproduced in any form, unless otherwise stated, in which case reproduction is limited to the use of the purchaser. The written instructions, photographs, designs, projects, and patterns are intended for the personal, noncommercial use of the retail purchaser and are under federal copyright laws; they are not to be reproduced by any electronic, mechanical, or other means, including informational storage or retrieval systems, for commercial use. Permission is granted to photocopy patterns for the personal use of the retail purchaser. Attention teachers: Martingale & Company encourages you to use this book for teaching, subject to the restrictions stated above.

The information in this book is presented in good faith, but no warranty is given nor results guaranteed. Since Martingale & Company has no control over choice of materials or procedures, the company assumes no responsibility for the use of this information.

Printed in China
12 11 10 09 08 07        8 7 6 5 4 3 2 1

**Library of Congress Cataloging-in-Publication Data**
Library of Congress Control Number: 2007009510

ISBN: 978-1-56477-743-0

## Credits

President & CEO: *Tom Wierzbicki*
Publisher: *Jane Hamada*
Editorial Director: *Mary V. Green*
Managing Editor: *Tina Cook*
Technical Editor: *Darra Williamson*
Copy Editor: *Melissa Bryan*
Design Director: *Stan Green*
Assistant Design Director: *Regina Girard*
Illustrator: *Adrienne Smitke*
Cover Designer: *Regina Girard*
Text Designer: *Trina Craig*
Photographer: *Brent Kane*

## Acknowledgments

I WOULD LIKE to thank my dream team:

My husband, Piet van den Eeden, for letting me follow all my crazy dreams and for keeping my computer in working shape at all times.

My mother, Topey Vosters, for always believing in me and for helping me make these mini quilts.

My friend Willy Trivière, for checking and translating my English and for all her valuable advice.

My family, Ansje, Willem, Nikki, and Teuntje Vosters, for all their support.

Martingale & Company, for giving me the opportunity again to do what I love most—designing and quilting!

Patchwork Promotions in Leende, for putting wonderful Hoffman fabrics at my disposal and for their encouragement.

Angela van Nistelrooij from De Quiltpuzzel in Eindhoven, for sponsoring and encouraging me.

Else van Veluw, for driving throughout the Netherlands in search of the right fabric and for her reliable support.

Wilma Vosters, Truus Schepers, Colette Keuten, Ankie Koster, Henny van der Haar, Margot Damen, Bieke le Clair, Joke Jansen, Bineke van der Haar, Corrie Pluimert, Marina Fluit, Jessamy Thompson, Margreet Selcraig, Ans van de Boogaard, Jeanette Kasbergen, Erika Vriend, Ellie Maas, Melanie Schultz, and Helga Carter for always being there at the right moment!

Members of the quilt groups The Blazing Stars, De Pientere Pitters, Quiltned, De Quiltkletsers, and all the ladies of the "quiltpagina prikbord."

## Mission Statement

Dedicated to providing quality products and service to inspire creativity.

# Contents

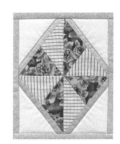

# How to Make These Quilts

THESE MINI QUILTS are surprisingly easy to make. You no longer need to sew tiny blocks together; these quilts are assembled by paper piecing parts (usually, but not always, rows)—sometimes with sashing in between or with a border all around. For example, the quilt illustrated below consists of only eight parts. As you make these individual parts, you sew them together. By the time you've added the last part, your quilt top is finished, *including borders and sashing.*

Paper piecing requires that you place your fabrics on the unmarked side of the paper foundation; as a result, the final pieced design appears as a reverse, or mirror, image of the printed pattern. Parts are divided into sections, each numbered according to the order in which it should be pieced. As you look through the various foundation patterns, you'll notice that sometimes position 1 appears at the top of a row, while in the next row position 1 appears at the bottom. This will help you remember to press the seam allowances in opposite directions from part to part, thus eliminating bulk when you begin sewing the parts together.

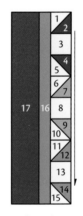

Part A.
Press seam
allowances down.

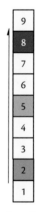

Part B.
Press seam
allowances up.

## RESIZING PATTERNS

*Perhaps the pattern that you like best isn't shown in the exact size you need for your quilt hanger or your decorating idea. In that case, you can easily resize the pattern by enlarging or reducing it on almost any copy machine. Let's say the pattern is given at 8", but you'd prefer it at 10". Divide 10 by 8 (the desired size by the original size); in this case, the outcome is 1.25. Multiply the outcome by 100; this gives you the exact percentage to adjust the copying machine (1.25 x 100 = 125%). Place the original 8" pattern on the copy machine, adjust the settings on the copier to enlarge the pattern by 125%, and you'll have a 10" pattern in a matter of seconds. See "Mini Tips" on page 11.*

# What Do You Need to Make These Quilts?

YOU DON'T NEED loads of fabric, nor do you need lots of fancy equipment to make these little quilts. You probably have most of what you need already on hand in your sewing room.

## Fabrics

Scraps, scraps, scraps! Like most quilters, you probably have a box full of scraps collected from your years of quiltmaking. Remainders from charm quilts, small leftover strips from Log Cabin designs and other projects—these scraps are perfect for making mini quilts. Here are a few guidelines for choosing fabrics for these mini quilts:

In general, avoid fabrics with large-scale prints. When cut into small pieces for a mini quilt, the design of a large-scale motif will be lost.

For similar reasons, stay away from fabrics with lots of open space between the printed motifs—save these for your larger projects. Cutting an open, airy print into small pieces will cause it to read as little splotches of color and print here and there, making the overall quilt design less distinct.

Be sure to choose fabrics in values that work well together. You'll quickly discover that a fabric's value—that is, its relative lightness or darkness—becomes increasingly important as your bits of fabric get smaller. Therefore, it's crucial to select fabrics with contrast that will be easily recognizable in small bits.

If you finish your mini quilt with the "birthing method" (page 9), it's best to use the same fabric for the backing as for the outer border so that you won't have a different color showing up at the edge of your quilt.

## Foundation Material

Use your favorite foundation material for these projects. There are several types of materials I like, particularly plain copy paper or other paper I can tear away easily; a lightweight nonfusible interfacing; and a product called Fun-Dation. Your local quilt store can advise you about the latest foundation materials.

## Batting

Do you have a box full of batting leftovers? You can use them now! I recommend that you use a thin batting, such as Hobbs Cotton; a thick batting is just too much for these little quilts. However, if need be, you can split thicker batting into two layers by peeling it apart.

### MINI TIP

*To test how fabrics will "read" in your mini quilt, cut a 1" square of each fabric you plan to use, place the squares on your design wall, and take a few steps back. From a distance, the differences in value will become more apparent while the distraction of color differences will diminish.*

### MINI TIP

*Do you intend to use your mini quilt in a doll-house or as a doll's blanket? If so, you might skip the filler layer altogether, or use flannel for that layer instead of batting. The resulting quilt will be nice and supple, and it will drape easily on the doll's bed.*

# How to Paper Piece These Quilts

FOR EACH QUILT, I provide specific cutting instructions for sashing (if applicable), borders, backing, and binding. Cut these pieces first to make best use of your fabric.

To make the mini quilts in this book, you'll use seam allowances of two different widths. When assembling the parts, rather than using the traditional ¼" seam allowance, you'll trim to ⅛" to reduce bulk. When joining the parts to complete the quilt, you'll maintain a ¼" seam allowance.

←—⅛" seam allowance

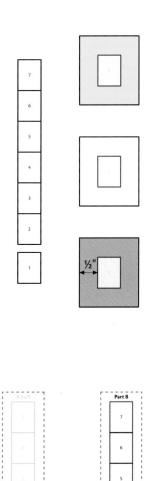

1.  Copy or trace the pattern(s) carefully onto the foundation material you have selected. If you are tracing, use a ruler and a pencil to draw the lines as straight as possible. Transfer the position numbers and the part letters onto the foundation as well. Notice that for asymmetrical parts, the pattern is a mirror image of the block design, since the fabrics will be stitched to the unmarked side of the foundation.

2.  To cut the fabric pieces for the quilt, make an extra copy of the pattern and cut it apart along the lines separating each numbered section. Pin each numbered section, printed side down, on the right side of the appropriate fabric. This allows you to see the fabric so you can isolate a particular motif, such as a little flower, that you might like to include. Roughly cut out the fabric shape, adding about ½" around the outline of the paper pattern as shown above right.

3.  Remove the paper pattern and then place the fabric piece for position 1 right side up on the unmarked side of the foundation, making sure the fabric overlaps position 1 by at least ¼" on all sides. Pin the fabric to the foundation from the marked side as shown at lower right.

4. Continuing to work from the unmarked side of the foundation, place the fabric for position 2 right sides together with the pinned fabric 1 piece, making sure that one fabric edge extends past the line between positions 1 and 2 by at least ¼".

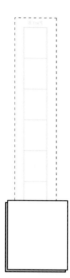

5. Secure the fabric 2 piece in place from the marked side of the foundation by pinning directly on the line between positions 1 and 2. Turn the foundation back over to the unmarked side and flip fabric 2 open so it covers position 2. Position 2 and any adjacent outer edges of the foundation should be completely covered.

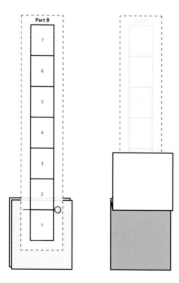

6. Set your sewing machine for a short stitch length (approximately 15 to 20 stitches per inch). Remove the pin from the sewing line and reposition it so it will not interfere with your stitching. Working

from the marked side of the foundation, sew directly on the line between positions 1 and 2, backstitching at the beginning and end of the line.

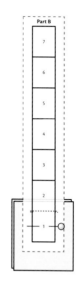

7. Fold the foundation back along the seam line you've just sewn and trim the fabric seam allowance to ⅛". I use scissors for this step because I find them easier on my wrist, elbow, and shoulder. You can use a rotary cutter if you prefer.

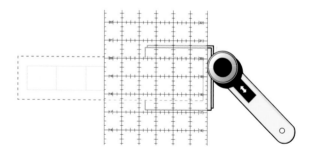

8. Working from the fabric side, finger-press or use an iron to press fabric 2 into place, flattening the seam.

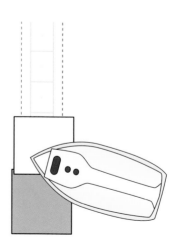

9.  Continue adding the fabric pieces in numerical order as described in the previous steps. After the final piece of the part has been sewn, trim along the dashed lines on the outer edge of the completed part.

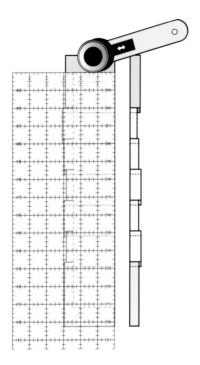

10. Press each part as you complete it and join the various parts of the design as soon as you finish them, pressing as you go. This minimizes the chance that you will sew them together upside down or in the wrong order. At the same time, you can check to see if the colors are placed correctly. Pressing arrows are included in the diagram for each quilt. In general, press the seam allowance toward the least bulky side. If both units are equally bulky, press the seam allowance open.

Press this way.        Press open.

To assemble the parts, refer to the project instructions for the quilt-top assembly order. Place adjacent sections right sides together and pin along the edges of the foundations. Open the parts to be sure they match correctly, reposition the pins so they do not interfere with your sewing, and sew the parts together along the edges of the foundations. Press as shown in the project assembly diagram.

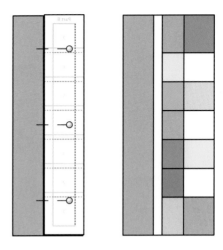

11. When the quilt top is complete, you may—if you wish—carefully tear away the foundation material.

## Mini Tip

*When I sew the various parts together with the foundation papers still in place, I always sew just outside the outermost drawn line. Experience has taught me that when you sew exactly on the line, the block turns out a bit too small. The more pieces involved, the more important this becomes. Even the smallest fraction of a difference multiplied over six seams quickly becomes ¼" or more!*

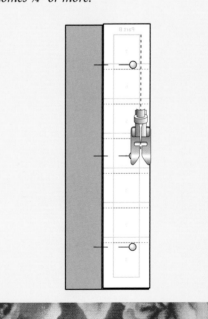

# Finishing Techniques

SOME OF THE QUILTS in this book are finished with binding, while others are layered right sides together, stitched around the outside edges with an opening left for turning, and then turned right side out, after which the opening is stitched closed by hand. (This latter method is called the "birthing method"!) Both finishing techniques are described in this section.

## The Birthing Method

Once you have sewn the parts together to finish the quilt top—including sashings and borders—it's time to layer the top, the batting, and the backing. I suggest you make the backing from the same material as the outer border to avoid a different color peeking out around the edges.

1. Measure your quilt and cut a piece of thin batting approximately ½" smaller than your quilt both crosswise and lengthwise. Set the batting aside for now.

2. Center the quilt top (right side down) on the backing fabric (right side up). Pin the layers together and trim the backing if necessary so it is ½" larger than the quilt top on all sides. Sew around the perimeter of the quilt top ¼" from the raw edges, leaving a wide opening on one short side as shown above right.

3. Cut the backing even with the raw edges of the quilt top. Trim the corners as shown at center right; you'll have less bulk to deal with and the corners will be neater.

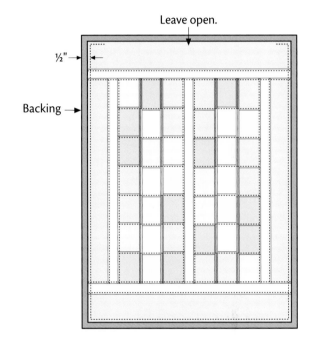

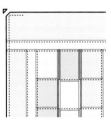

## MINI TIP

*When you sew the layers together, be sure to leave an opening large enough that you can turn the quilt and insert the batting easily. If necessary, use barbecue tongs to help with these steps.*

4.  Turn the quilt right side out and press, particularly along the edges. Insert the batting inside the quilt, between the quilt top and the backing. Pin the layers together to prevent shifting, fold the raw edges of the opening inward, and stitch the opening closed by hand. Remove the pins and you are ready to start quilting!

# Traditional Single-Fold Binding

For quilts of this size, a double-fold French binding would be a bit out of proportion. A simple single-fold binding will do.

1.  Cut the backing fabric and a piece of thin batting approximately 1" larger than the quilt top. Lay out the backing, wrong side up. Center the batting on top of the backing, and then the finished top, right side up, over the batting and backing. Smooth the layers, and then baste them together with safety pins.

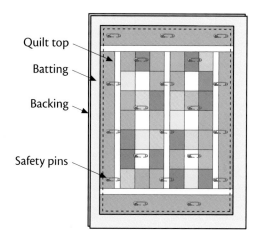

2.  Quilt the quilt sandwich as desired.

3.  Trim the backing and batting even with the quilt top.

4.  Cut 1¼"-wide strips across the width of the binding fabric. Stitch the strips together as shown to make one long strip. Press the seams open.

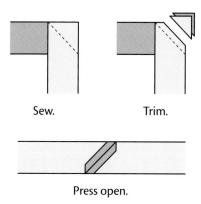

Sew.    Trim.

Press open.

5.  Press the beginning end of the binding strip at a 45° angle as shown. Beginning several inches from a corner of the quilt, pin the binding strip along one edge of the right side of the quilt top, keeping the beginning fold intact. Stitch the binding to the quilt with a ¼" seam allowance, ending ¼" from the first corner. Backstitch and remove the quilt from the machine.

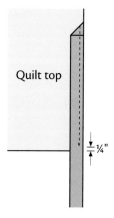

6.  Turn the quilt to prepare for sewing the next edge. Fold the binding up at a 45° angle as shown. Keeping the angled fold secure, fold the binding back down, parallel with the new edge of the quilt top. Beginning at the fold, stitch the binding in place, ending ¼" from the next corner. Repeat to sew the remaining corners.

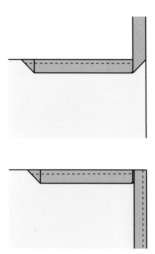

7.  Stop stitching when you are approximately 2" from the starting point. Overlap the end of the binding strip with the beginning of the binding strip by about 1½". Cut off the excess and finish stitching the binding strip to the edge of the quilt.

1½" overlap

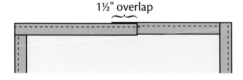

8.  Fold the binding over the raw edges of the quilt to the back. Turn under the raw edges of the binding and slipstitch in place, mitering the corners.

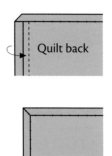

Quilt back

### Mini Tips

*Don't forget to check the paper orientation and size before printing; the pattern needs to fit the paper! Use larger paper for oversized patterns.*

*Always test the photocopier for possible distortion before enlarging or reducing, or before making multiple copies of any printed pattern. Make a single copy at the original size first; then place the copy over the original and hold them both up to the light to make sure they match.*

# Purple Dream

**Finished Quilt: 8½" x 10"**

*Sometimes at a quilt show, you see a quilt with a color combination that strikes you immediately. On the spot you decide to make a quilt in those same colors . . . someday. But you know what happens. You store so many quilts away in your "someday" memory, you'd need at least 150 years to make them all! The solution? Make a mini quilt! This little quilt fulfilled one of my color-combination fantasies. At least one of my someday dreams has come true!*

# Materials

- 1 fat quarter of dark purple print for outer border, backing, and binding
- 11" x 11" scrap of coordinating batik print for inner border and sashing
- 10" x 17" *total* of assorted green print scraps for patchwork strips
- 10" x 17" *total* of assorted purple print scraps for patchwork strips
- 9½" x 11" piece of batting

# Cutting

**From the coordinating batik print, cut:**
4 strips, 1½" x 8"
2 strips, 1½" x 9½"

**From the dark purple print, cut:**
2 strips, 2" x 9½"
2 strips, 2" x 8"
1 rectangle, 9½" x 11"
3 strips, 1¼" x 20"

# Assembly and Finishing

1.  Copy or trace the foundation patterns on pages 14–15 onto your preferred foundation material. Make one copy each of parts A, B, and C, and two copies of part D.

2.  Referring to "How to Paper Piece These Quilts" on page 6, paper piece parts A–D. Refer to the quilt diagram below and the project photo as a guide for fabric placement. As you complete the parts, assemble the quilt top as follows:
    - Join A and C to opposite sides of B.
    - Join the D parts to the top and bottom of the quilt.

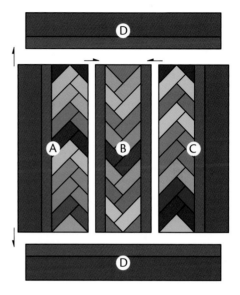

3.  Referring to "Traditional Single-Fold Binding" on page 10, layer the 9½" x 11" dark purple backing piece, the batting, and the quilt top; baste. Quilt as desired. Bind the quilt edges with the 1¼" x 20" dark purple strips.

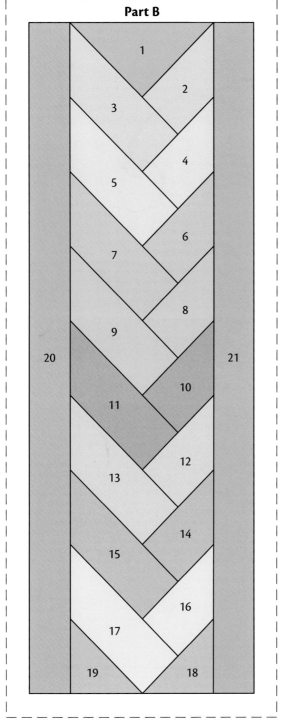

**Part B**

Make 1 copy.

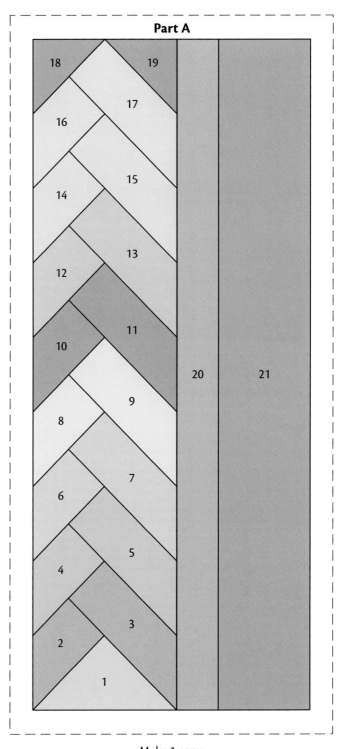

**Part A**

Make 1 copy.

**Part D**

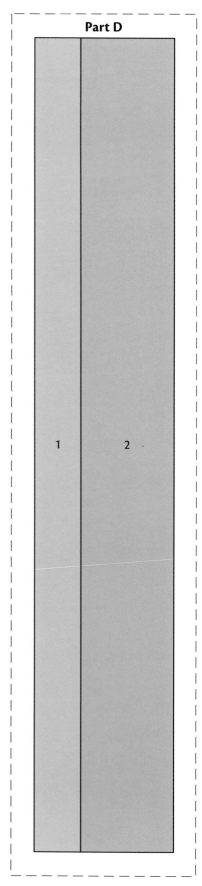

Make 2 copies.

**Part C**

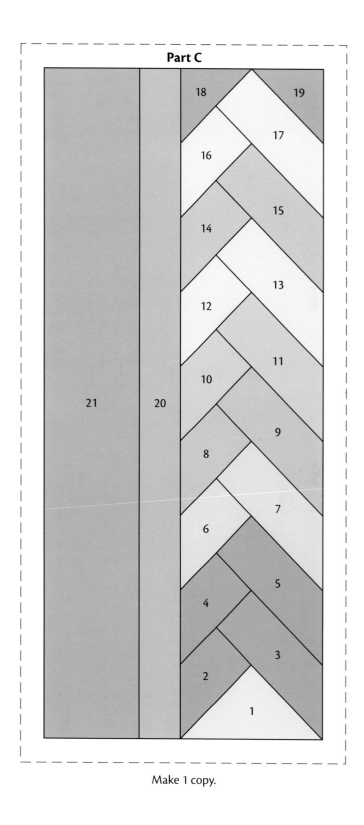

Make 1 copy.

# Shoofly Mini

**Finished Quilt: 7" x 8½"**

*This mini quilt was the start of it all for me. Since I made this quilt, I have made a number of others in different color variations to give away as presents. Each one has been a huge success, showing how much a recipient appreciates a gift with a personal touch.*

Skill Level: Advanced

# Materials

- 1 fat quarter of red print for outer border, corner blocks, backing, and optional binding
- 15" x 15" scrap of white-on-white print for block backgrounds
- 10" x 12" scrap of green print for inner border, sashing, and corner blocks
- 6" x 6" scrap *each* of 6 assorted prints for blocks
- 7" x 8½" piece of batting

# Cutting

**From the green print, cut:**

3 strips, 1½" x 7"

2 strips, 1½" x 5½"

2 squares, 3" x 3"; cut each square once diagonally to yield 4 half-square triangles

**From the red print, cut:**

2 strips, 2" x 7"

2 strips, 2" x 5½"

2 squares, 3" x 3"; cut each square once diagonally to yield 4 half-square triangles

1 rectangle, 8" x 9½"

2 strips, 1¼" x 20" (for optional binding)

# Assembly and Finishing

The quilt shown on page 16 is finished using the birthing method described on page 9. If you prefer a binding, refer to "Traditional Single-Fold Binding" on page 10. For that method, use an 8" x 9½" piece of batting, prepare the quilt for quilting as instructed, and use the 1¼" x 20" red strips to bind the quilt edges.

1. Copy or trace the foundation patterns on pages 18–19 onto your preferred foundation material. Make one copy each of parts A, B, C, D, E, and F, and two copies of part G.

2. Referring to "How to Paper Piece These Quilts" on page 6, paper piece parts A–G. Refer to the quilt diagram below and the project photo as a guide for fabric placement. As you complete the parts, assemble the quilt top as follows:
   - Join A to B (AB).
   - Join AB to C (ABC).
   - Join ABC to D (ABCD).
   - Join ABCD to E (ABCDE).
   - Join ABCDE to F.
   - Join the G parts to the top and bottom of the quilt.

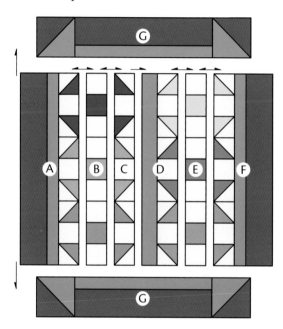

3. Referring to "The Birthing Method" on page 9, prepare the quilt sandwich (quilt top, batting, and 8" x 9½" red print backing piece) for quilting. Quilt as desired.

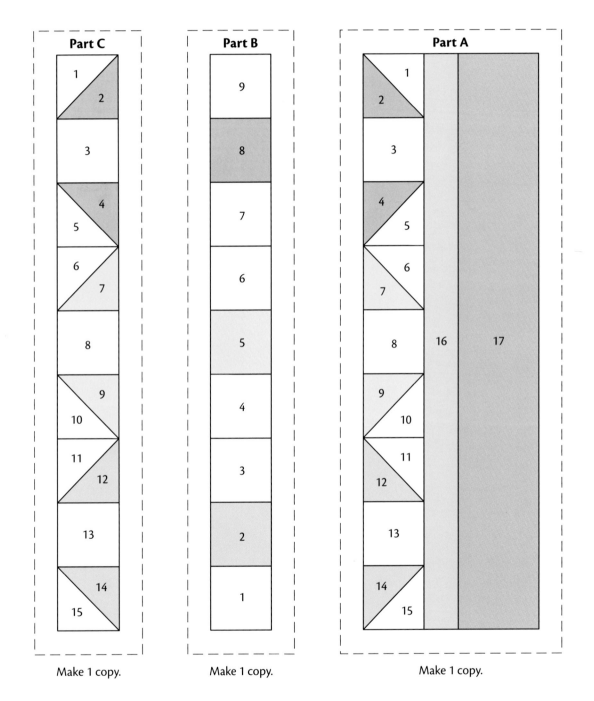

Make 1 copy.          Make 1 copy.          Make 1 copy.

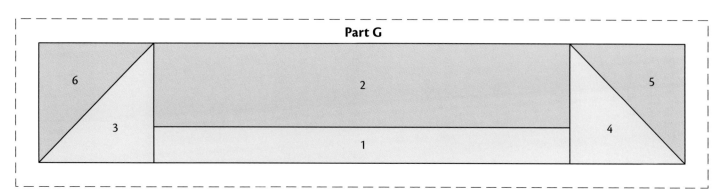

Make 2 copies.

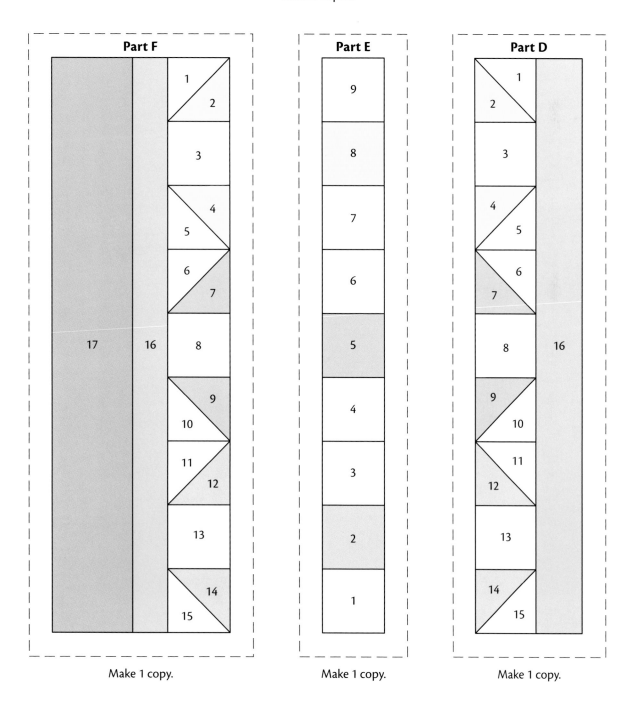

Make 1 copy.          Make 1 copy.          Make 1 copy.

# Grandma's Little Quilt

Finished Quilt: 5¾" x 7¾" (shown actual size)

This quilt hangs on my wall in a dark paper mat and a rustic wooden frame. It now has a vintage feel that's perfectly suited for a country interior. Old-fashioned buttons complete the look.

Skill Level: Advanced

## Materials

- 1 fat quarter of purple print for outer border, backing, and optional binding
- 15" x 15" *total* of assorted colorful scraps for patchwork rectangles
- 8" x 9" scrap of white-on-white print for sashing and inner border
- 5¾" x 7¾" piece of batting
- 6 heart-shaped buttons (optional)

## Cutting

**From the white-on-white print, cut:**
5 strips, 1¼" x 7"

**From the purple print, cut:**
4 strips, 1¾" x 7"
1 rectangle, 7" x 9"
2 strips, 1¼" x 20" (for optional binding)

## Assembly and Finishing

The quilt shown on page 20 is finished using the birthing method described on page 9. If you prefer a binding, refer to "Traditional Single-Fold Binding" on page 10. For that method, use a 7" x 9" piece of batting, prepare the quilt for quilting as instructed, and use the 1¼" x 20" purple strips to bind the quilt edges.

1.  Copy or trace the foundation patterns on pages 22–23 onto your preferred foundation material. Make one copy each of parts A, B, C, D, E, and F, and two copies of part G.

2.  Referring to "How to Paper Piece These Quilts" on page 6, paper piece parts A–G. Refer to the quilt diagram below and the project photo as a guide for fabric placement. As you complete the parts, assemble the quilt top as follows:
    - Join A to B (AB).
    - Join AB to C (ABC).
    - Join ABC to D (ABCD).
    - Join ABCD to E (ABCDE).
    - Join ABCDE to F.
    - Join the G parts to the top and bottom of the quilt.

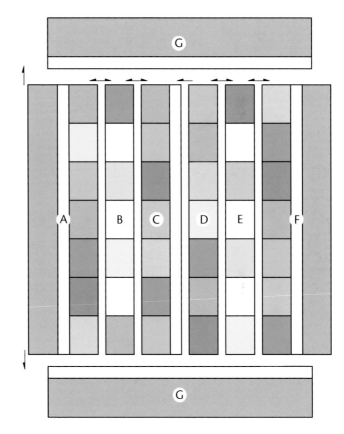

3.  Referring to "The Birthing Method" on page 9, prepare the quilt sandwich (quilt top, batting, and 7" x 9" purple print backing piece) for quilting. Quilt as desired and, if you wish, attach six heart-shaped buttons to parts B and E as shown in the project photo.

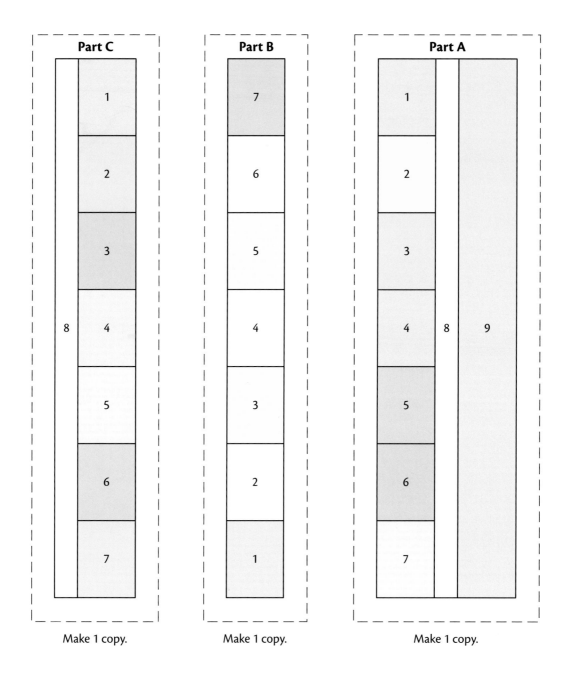

Make 1 copy.          Make 1 copy.          Make 1 copy.

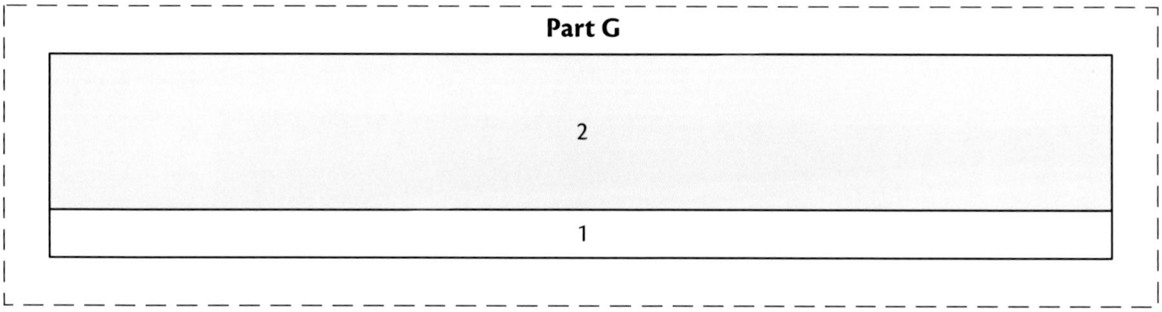

**Part G**

| 2 |
|---|
| 1 |

Make 2 copies.

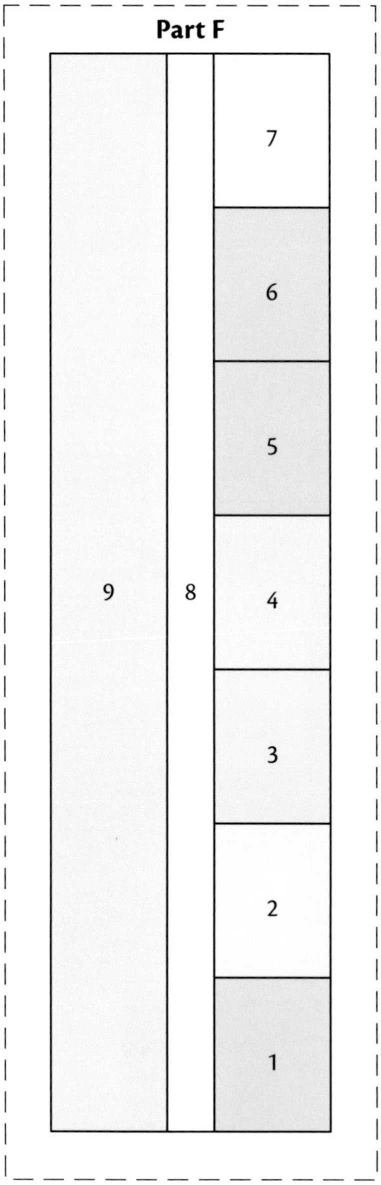

**Part F**

| 9 | 8 | 7 |
| | | 6 |
| | | 5 |
| | | 4 |
| | | 3 |
| | | 2 |
| | | 1 |

Make 1 copy.

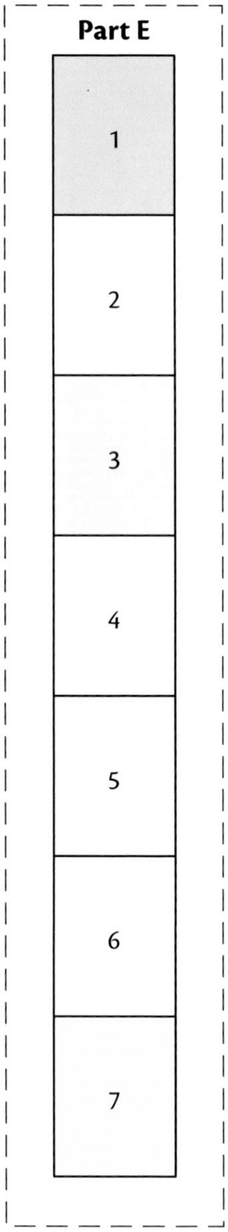

**Part E**

| 1 |
|---|
| 2 |
| 3 |
| 4 |
| 5 |
| 6 |
| 7 |

Make 1 copy.

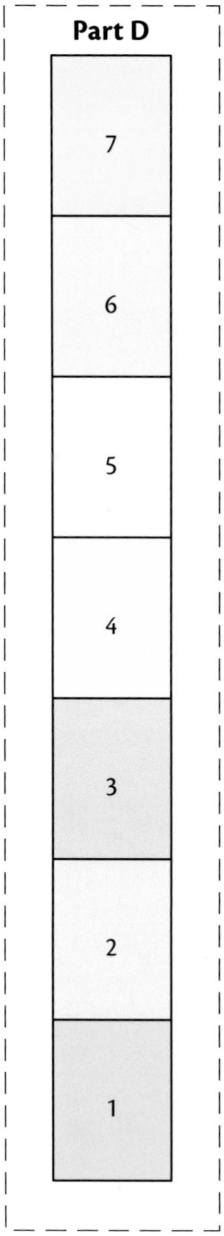

**Part D**

| 7 |
|---|
| 6 |
| 5 |
| 4 |
| 3 |
| 2 |
| 1 |

Make 1 copy.

# Stained-Glass Quilt

**Finished Quilt: 6¾" x 8"**

*This project with the look of stained glass is also attractive in small-scale, country-style prints or when displayed in a group of three mini quilts, each with its own color variations.*

Skill Level: Advanced

# Materials

- 1 fat quarter of black solid fabric for border, sashing, backing, and optional binding
- 12" x 20" *total* of assorted brightly colored marbled or hand-dyed scraps for blocks and corner squares
- 6¾" x 8" piece of batting

# Cutting

**From the black solid fabric, cut:**
2 strips, 2" x 7"
2 strips, 2" x 5¾"
3 strips, 1¼" x 7"
16 rectangles, 1¼" x 2"
1 rectangle, 7¾" x 9"
2 strips, 1¼" x 20" (for optional binding)

**From *each* of 4 different brightly colored marbled or hand-dyed scraps, cut:**
1 square, 2" x 2"

# Assembly and Finishing

The quilt shown on page 24 is finished using the birthing method described on page 9. If you prefer a binding, refer to "Traditional Single-Fold Binding" on page 10. For that method, use a 7¾" x 9" piece of batting, prepare the quilt for quilting as instructed, and use the 1¼" x 20" black strips to bind the quilt edges.

1. Copy or trace the foundation patterns on pages 26–27 onto your preferred foundation material. Make one copy each of parts A, B, C, D, E, and F.

2. Referring to "How to Paper Piece These Quilts" on page 6, paper piece parts A–F. Refer to the quilt diagram below and the project photo as a guide for fabric placement. As you complete the parts, assemble the quilt top as follows:
   - Join A to B (AB).
   - Join AB to C (ABC).
   - Join ABC to D (ABCD).
   - Join E to the top of the quilt and F to the bottom of the quilt.

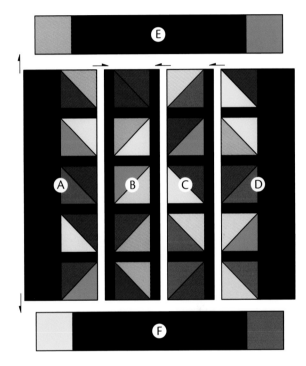

3. Referring to "The Birthing Method" on page 9, prepare the quilt sandwich (quilt top, batting, and 7¾" x 9" black backing piece) for quilting. Quilt as desired.

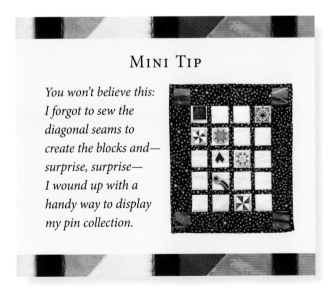

## MINI TIP

*You won't believe this: I forgot to sew the diagonal seams to create the blocks and— surprise, surprise— I wound up with a handy way to display my pin collection.*

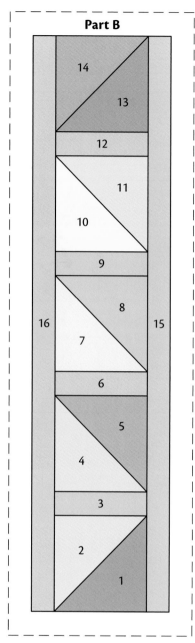

**Part B**

Make 1 copy.

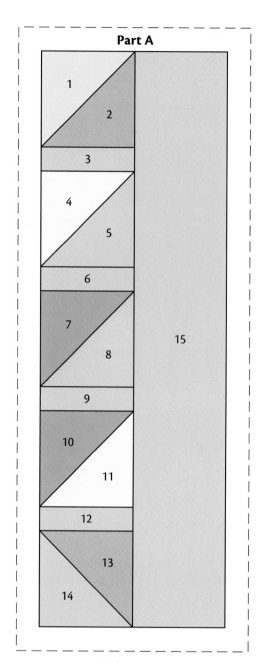

**Part A**

Make 1 copy.

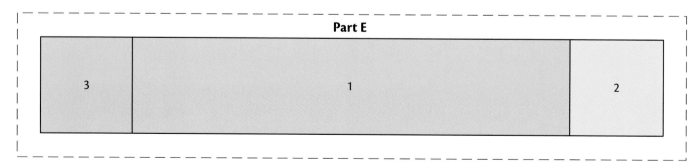

**Part E**

Make 1 copy.

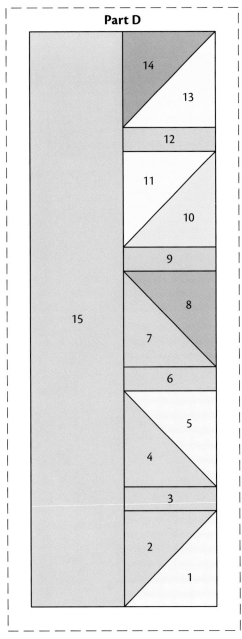

Make 1 copy.

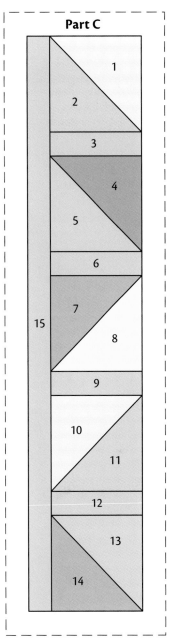

Make 1 copy.

**Part F**

| 3 | 1 | 2 |

Make 1 copy.

# Crazy Quilt

**Finished Quilt: 10" x 12"**

*Of course I just had to have a crazy quilt in my book. This one is super easy and makes up in a jiffy. It's a very useful little item: try using it as a candle mat on a sideboard.*

Skill Level: Intermediate

# Materials

- 20" x 20" piece of green print for outer border, crazy pieces, backing, and binding
- 18" x 22" *total* of assorted green, red, and pink floral prints for crazy pieces
- 12" x 22" scrap of cream print for background, middle border, and corner blocks
- 15" x 15" scrap of red print for inner border, sashing, crazy pieces, and corner blocks
- 11" x 13" piece of batting

# Cutting

**From the red print, cut:**
4 strips, 1½" x 7"
2 strips, 1½" x 10"
2 strips, 1½" x 8"
2 squares, 3½" x 3½"; cut each square once diagonally to yield 4 half-square triangles

**From the cream print, cut:**
4 rectangles, 4" x 6"
2 strips, 1½" x 10"
2 strips, 1½" x 8"
2 squares, 3½" x 3½"; cut each square once diagonally to yield 4 half-square triangles

**From the green print, cut:**
2 strips, 1¾" x 10"
2 strips, 1¾" x 8"
1 rectangle, 11" x 13"
3 strips, 1¼" x 20"

# Assembly and Finishing

1. Copy or trace the foundation patterns on pages 30–32 onto your preferred foundation material. Make one copy each of parts A and B, and two copies of part C.

2. Referring to "How to Paper Piece These Quilts" on page 6, paper piece parts A–C. Refer to the quilt diagram below and the project photo as a guide for fabric placement. As you complete the parts, assemble the quilt top as follows:
   - Join A to B.
   - Join the C parts to the top and bottom of the quilt.

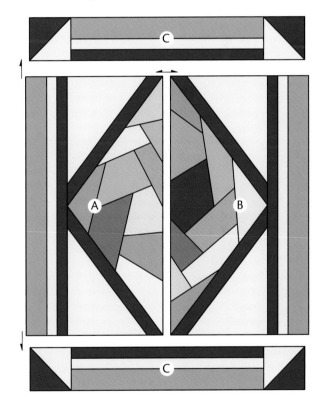

3. Referring to "Traditional Single-Fold Binding" on page 10, layer the 11" x 13" green print backing piece, the batting, and the quilt top; baste. Quilt as desired. Bind the quilt edges with the 1¼" x 20" green print strips.

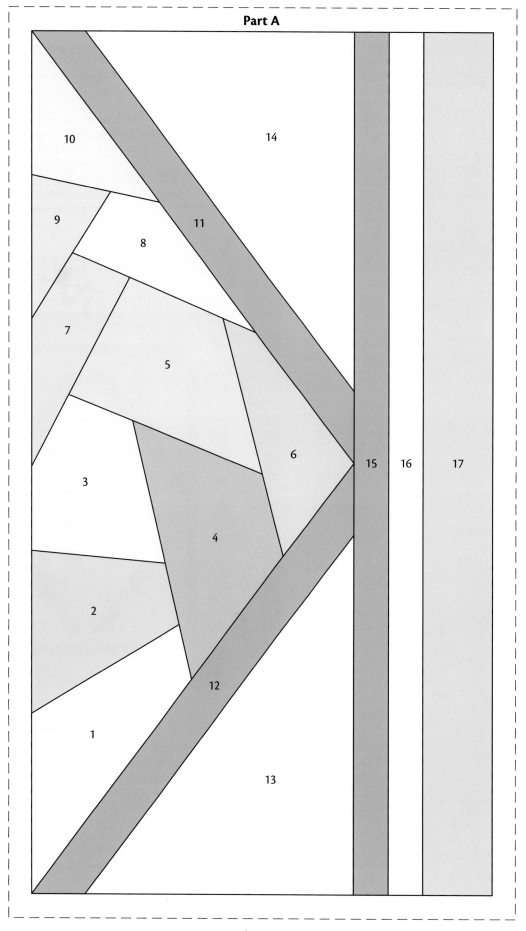

**Part A**

Make 1 copy.

**Part B**

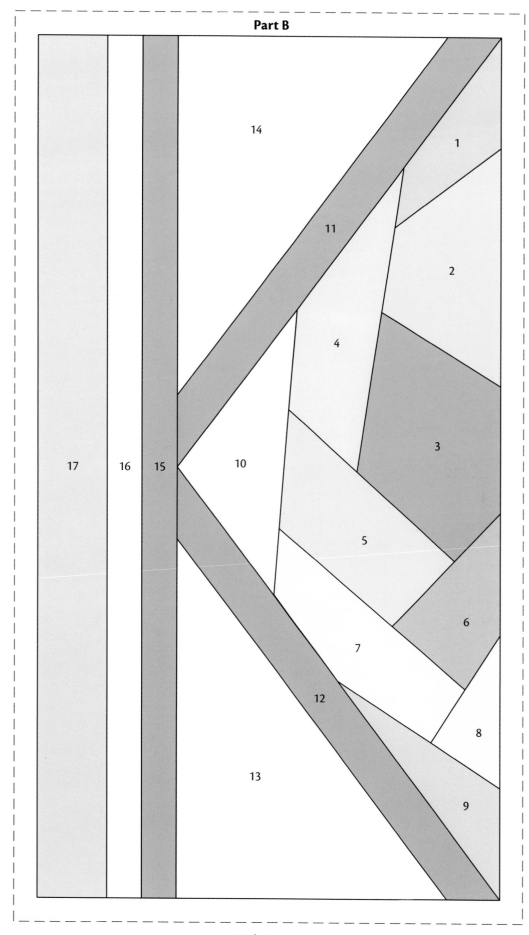

Make 1 copy.

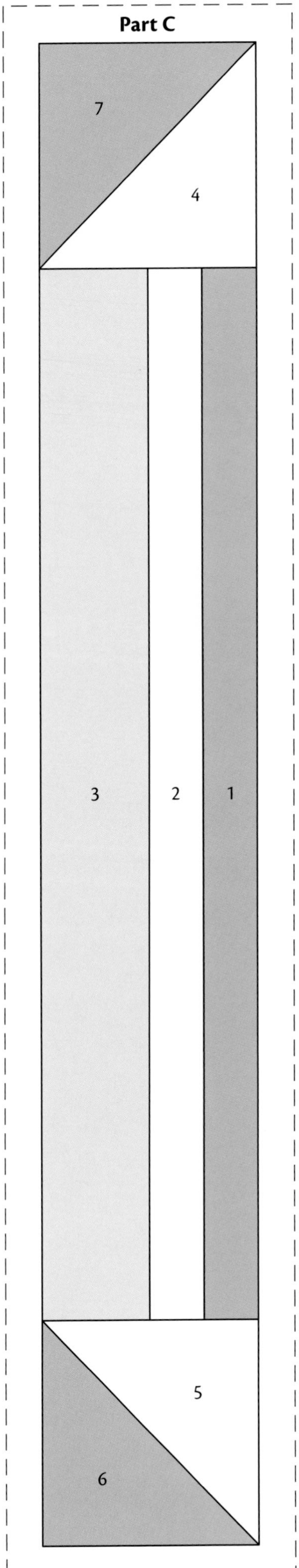

**Part C**

7

4

3    2    1

Make 2 copies.

5

6

Part C

# Scrappy Quilt

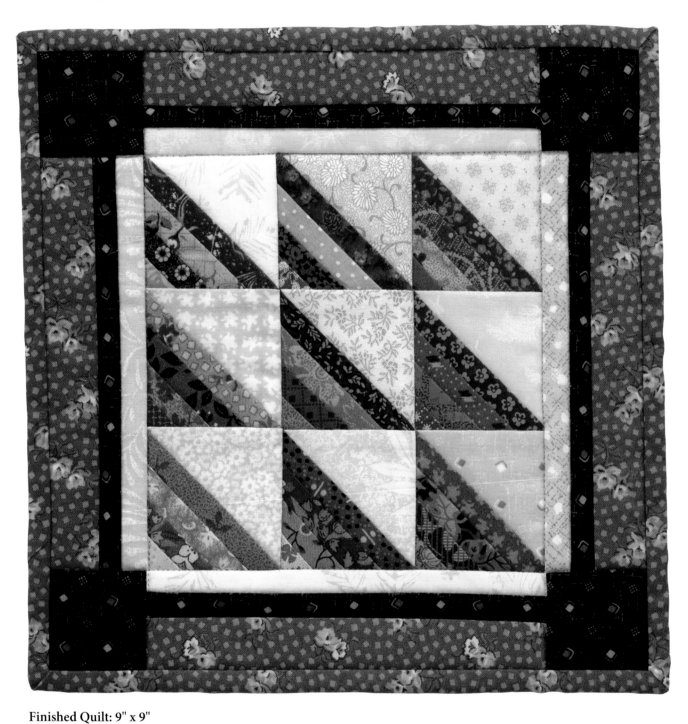

**Finished Quilt: 9" x 9"**

*This traditional pattern looks nice in just about any fabric. It doesn't take long to sew it with my new method, so if you need to make a present, this is it!*

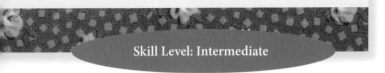

Skill Level: Intermediate

## Materials

- 1 fat quarter of dark red print for outer border, backing, and binding
- 18" x 22" *total* of assorted medium and dark print scraps for stripes
- 11" x 16" *total* of assorted cream print scraps for blocks and inner border
- 9" x 14" scrap of black print for middle border and corner blocks
- 10" x 10" piece of batting

## Cutting

**From the cream prints, cut a *total* of:**
4 strips, 1¼" x 7"

**From the black print, cut:**
4 strips, 1¼" x 7"
4 squares, 2½" x 2½"

**From the dark red print, cut:**
4 strips, 1¾" x 7"
1 square, 10" x 10"
3 strips, 1¼" x 20"

## Assembly and Finishing

1. Copy or trace the foundation patterns on pages 35–36 onto your preferred foundation material. Make one copy each of parts A, B, and C, and two copies of part D.

2. Referring to "How to Paper Piece These Quilts" on page 6, paper piece parts A–D. Refer to the quilt diagram below and the project photo on page 33 as a guide for fabric placement. As you complete the parts, assemble the quilt top as follows:
   - Join A and C to opposite sides of B.
   - Join the D parts to the top and bottom of the quilt.

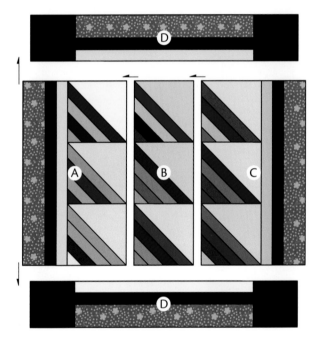

3. Referring to "Traditional Single-Fold Binding" on page 10, layer the 10" x 10" dark red print backing piece, the batting, and the quilt top; baste. Quilt as desired. Bind the quilt edges with the 1¼" x 20" dark red print strips.

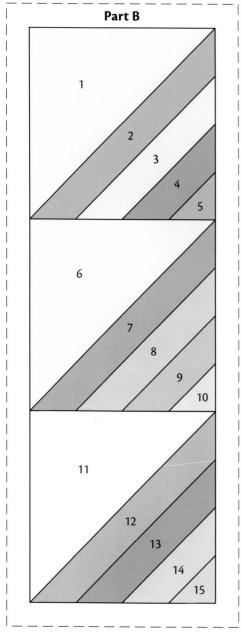

**Part B**

Make 1 copy.

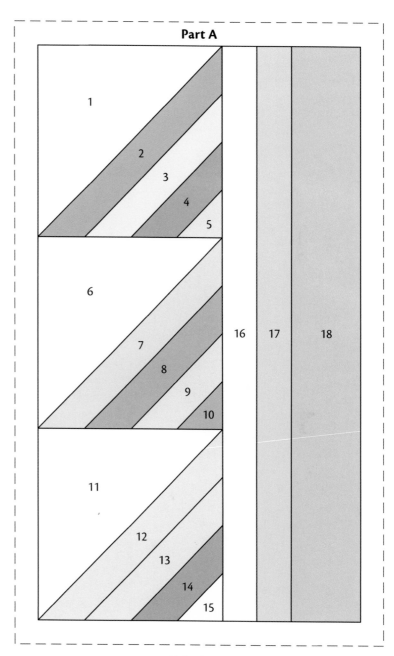

**Part A**

Make 1 copy.

**Part D**

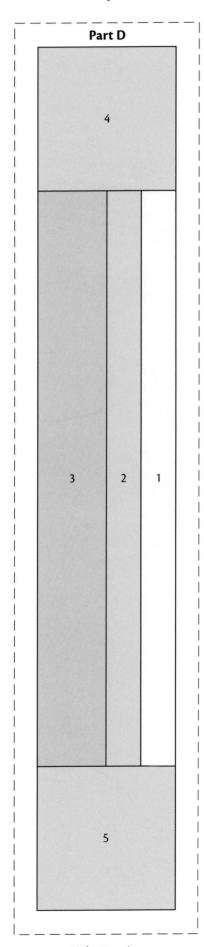

Make 2 copies.

**Part C**

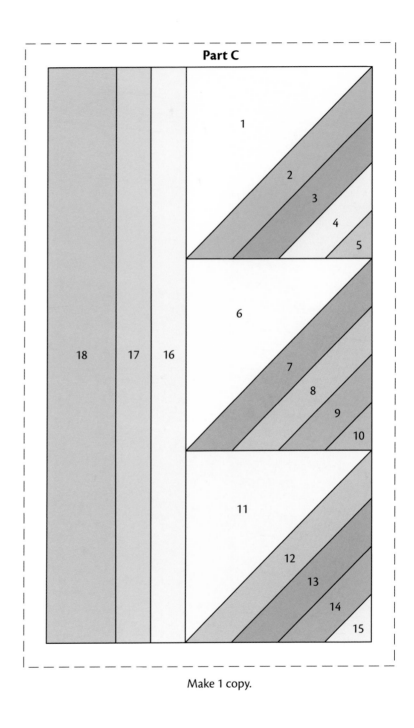

Make 1 copy.

# Spring Windmill

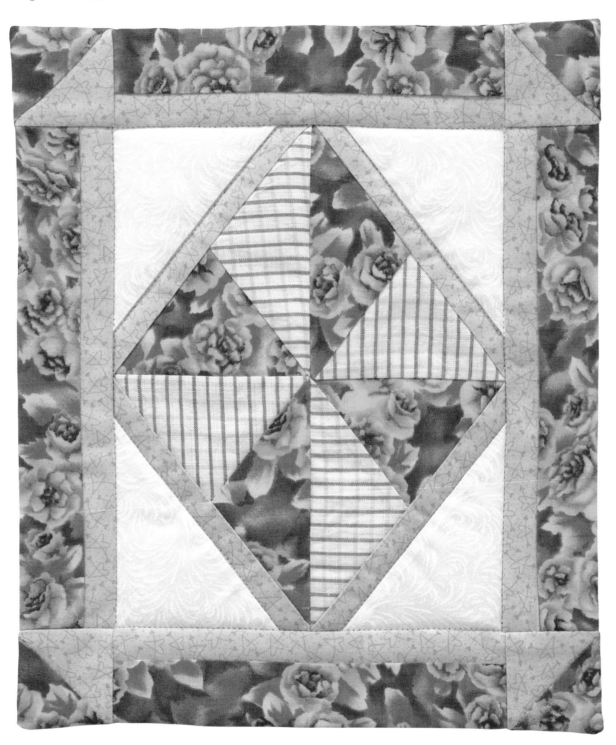

**Finished Quilt: 9" x 10½"**

*This quilt is constructed from slightly bigger pieces, making it perfect for holiday prints such as those available for Halloween, Christmas, or the Fourth of July (see the alternate version on page 38). All in all, it's a pattern with loads of possibilities.*

Skill Level: Intermediate

# Materials

- ½ yard of orange rose print for outer border, corner blocks, windmill blades, backing, and optional binding
- 13" x 14" scrap of light green print for inner border, corner blocks, and sashing
- 11" x 11" scrap of white-on-white print for quilt-center background
- 7" x 13" scrap of coordinating plaid fabric for windmill blades
- 9" x 10½" piece of batting

# Cutting

**From the light green print, cut:**

2 strips, 1½" x 8½"

2 strips, 1½" x 7"

2 squares, 3" x 3"; cut each square once diagonally to yield 4 half-square triangles

**From the orange rose print, cut:**

2 strips, 2" x 8½"

2 strips, 2" x 7"

2 squares, 3" x 3"; cut each square once diagonally to yield 4 half-square triangles

1 rectangle, 10" x 11½"

3 strips, 1¼" x 20" (for optional binding)

# Assembly and Finishing

The quilt shown on page 37 is finished using the birthing method described on page 9. If you prefer a binding, refer to "Traditional Single-Fold Binding" on page 10. For that method, use a 10" x 11½" piece of batting, prepare the quilt for quilting as instructed, and use the 1¼" x 20" orange rose print strips to bind the quilt edges.

1. Copy or trace the foundation patterns on page 39 onto your preferred foundation material. Make two copies each of parts A and B.

2. Referring to "How to Paper Piece These Quilts" on page 6, paper piece parts A and B. Refer to the quilt diagram below and the project photo on page 37 as a guide for fabric placement. As you complete the parts, assemble the quilt top as follows:
   - Lay out the two A parts, rotating one part 180°.
   - Join the two A parts.
   - Join the B parts to the top and bottom of the quilt.

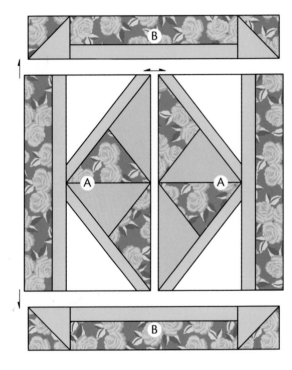

3. Referring to "The Birthing Method" on page 9, prepare the quilt sandwich (quilt top, batting, and 10" x 11½" orange rose print backing piece) for quilting. Quilt as desired.

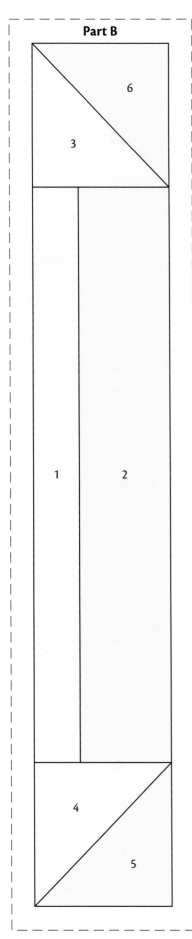

### Part B

6

3

1     2

4

5

Make 2 copies.

### Part A

8

5

4

3

9     10

2

1

6

7

Make 2 copies.

# Brown Pineapple

**Finished Quilt: 10½" x 13"**

*W*hen you first see this Pineapple quilt, you have to look really carefully to figure out how it is done. These are two half-pineapple blocks! Would you have guessed? This is another quilt that makes a great candle mat.

Skill Level: Intermediate

# Materials

- ½ yard *total* of assorted blue prints for outer border, corner pieces, pineapple triangles, backing, and optional binding
- 18" x 22" *total* of assorted cream print scraps for pineapple background strips
- 18" x 22" *total* of assorted brown print scraps for pineapple strips
- 8" x 13" scrap of brown print for inner border
- 10½" x 13" piece of batting

# Cutting

**From the brown print, cut:**
4 strips, 1½" x 11"
2 strips, 1½" x 9½"

**From the assorted blue prints, cut a *total* of:**
2 strips, 2" x 11"
2 strips, 2" x 9½"
4 rectangles, 2" x 2½"
1 rectangle, 11½" x 14"
3 strips, 1¼" x 20" (for optional binding)

# Assembly and Finishing

The quilt shown on page 40 is finished using the birthing method described on page 9. If you prefer a binding, refer to "Traditional Single-Fold Binding" on page 10. For that method, use an 11½" x 14" piece of batting, prepare the quilt for quilting as instructed, and use the 1¼" x 20" blue print strips to bind the quilt edges.

1. Copy or trace the foundation patterns on pages 42–43 onto your preferred foundation material, enlarging part B as instructed. Make two copies each of parts A and B.

2. Referring to "How to Paper Piece These Quilts" on page 6, paper piece parts A and B. Refer to the quilt diagram below and the project photo as a guide for fabric placement. As you complete the parts, assemble the quilt top as follows:
   - Lay out the two A parts, rotating one part 180°.
   - Join the two A parts.
   - Join the B parts to the top and bottom of the quilt.

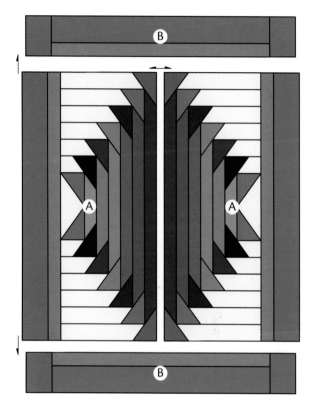

3. Referring to "The Birthing Method" on page 9, prepare the quilt sandwich (quilt top, batting, and 11½" x 14" blue print backing piece) for quilting. Quilt as desired.

*Try this quilt with a combination of Asian-inspired prints to create a completely different look.*

**Part B**

3

1    2

4

Enlarge part B 125%.
Make 2 copies.

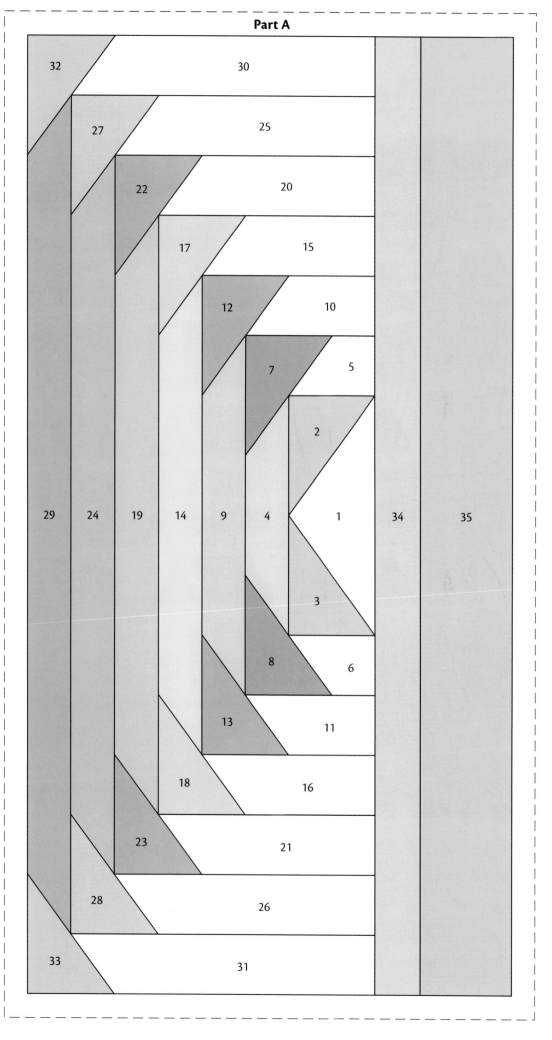

**Part A**

Pattern is full sized.
*Do not enlarge.*
Make 2 copies.

# Houses

**Finished Quilt: 8½" x 8½"**

*Everyone will admire this sweet little quilt. It looks far more difficult than it is, and it makes the ideal present for a housewarming party!*

**Skill Level: Advanced**

# Materials

- 1 fat quarter of cream print for house backgrounds
- 1 fat quarter of red polka-dot print for outer border, corner blocks, backing, and binding
- 8" x 9" scrap of red plaid for inner border
- 7" x 9" scrap of dark red print for middle border
- 6" x 6" scrap *each* of 9 different red prints for houses
- 9½" x 9½" piece of batting

# Cutting

**From the red plaid, cut:**
4 strips, 1½" x 7"

**From the dark red print, cut:**
4 strips, 1¼" x 7"

**From the red polka-dot print, cut:**
4 strips, 1½" x 7"
4 squares, 2¼" x 2¼"
1 square, 9½" x 9½"
3 strips, 1¼" x 20"

# Assembly and Finishing

1. Copy or trace the foundation patterns on pages 46–47 onto your preferred foundation material. Make one copy each of parts A and D and two copies each of parts B, C, and E.

2. Referring to "How to Paper Piece These Quilts" on page 6, paper piece parts A–E. Refer to the quilt diagram below and the project photo as a guide for fabric placement. As you complete the parts, assemble the quilt top as follows:
   - Join A to B (AB).
   - Join AB to C (ABC).
   - Join ABC to the remaining B (ABCB).
   - Join ABCB to the remaining C (ABCBC).
   - Join ABCBC to D.
   - Join the E pieces to the sides of the quilt.

3. Referring to "Traditional Single-Fold Binding" on page 10, layer the 9½" x 9½" red polka-dot backing piece, the batting, and the quilt top; baste. Quilt as desired. Bind the quilt edges with the 1¼" x 20" red polka-dot strips.

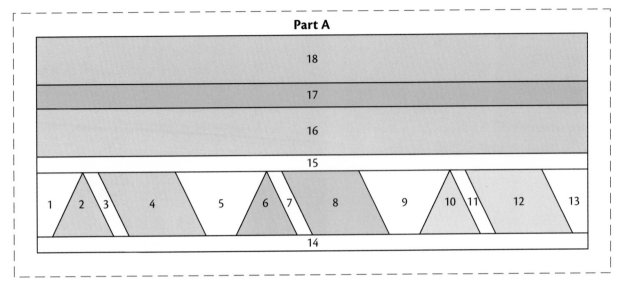

Make 1 copy.

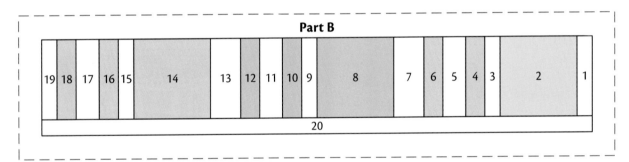

Make 2 copies.

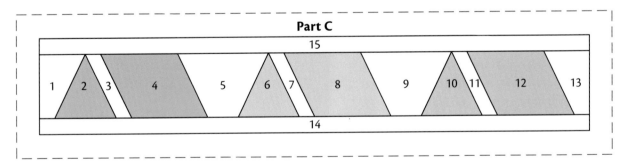

Make 2 copies.

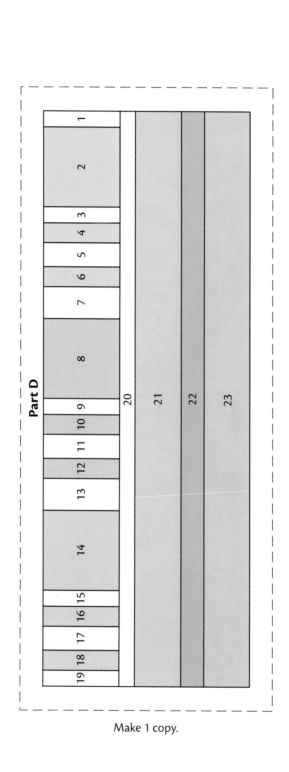

**Part D**

Make 1 copy.

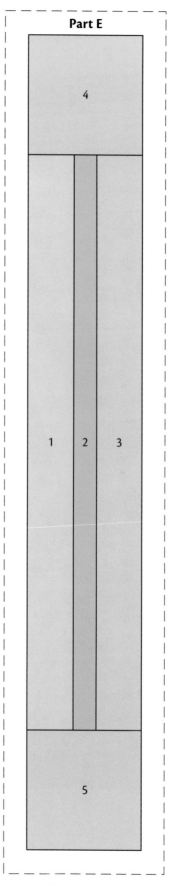

**Part E**

Make 2 copies.

# Christmas Joy

**Finished Quilt: 8" x 10"**

*Believe it or not, this festive quilt is made from just three parts! Make it for the holiday season to add a warm, welcoming touch to your front porch, front door, or entryway.*

Skill Level: Intermediate

# Materials

- 1 fat quarter of red holly print for tree trim, inner sashing, inner border, corner blocks, and binding
- 1 fat quarter of green holly print for outer border, corner blocks, and backing
- 16" x 18" scrap of white-and-green holly print for quilt-center background
- 6" x 9" scrap of cream print for tree background
- 4" x 8" scrap of green print for tree
- 2" x 2¾" scrap of brown print for trunk
- 9" x 11" piece of batting

# Cutting

**From the red holly print, cut:**
4 strips, 1½" x 3½"
2 strips, 1½" x 8"
2 strips, 1½" x 6"
2 strips, 1½" x 5½"
6 strips, 1½" x 4½"
2 squares, 3" x 3"; cut each square once diagonally to
    yield 4 half-square triangles
3 strips, 1¼" x 20"

**From the white-and-green holly print, cut:**
2 strips, 1½" x 8"
2 strips, 1½" x 6"

**From the green holly print, cut:**
2 strips, 1½" x 8"
2 strips, 1½" x 6"
4 strips, 1½" x 4½"
4 strips, 1½" x 3½"
2 squares, 3" x 3"; cut each square once diagonally to
    yield 4 half-square triangles
1 rectangle, 9" x 11"

# Assembly and Finishing

1. Copy or trace the foundation patterns on pages 50–51 onto your preferred foundation material. Make one copy of part A and two copies of part B.

2. Referring to "How to Paper Piece These Quilts" on page 6, paper piece parts A and B. Refer to the quilt diagram below and the project photo as a guide for fabric placement. As you complete the parts, assemble the quilt top as follows:
   - Join the B parts to opposite sides of A.

3. Referring to "Traditional Single-Fold Binding" on page 10, layer the 9" x 11" green holly backing piece, the batting, and the quilt top; baste. Quilt as desired. Bind the quilt edges with the 1¼" x 20" red holly strips.

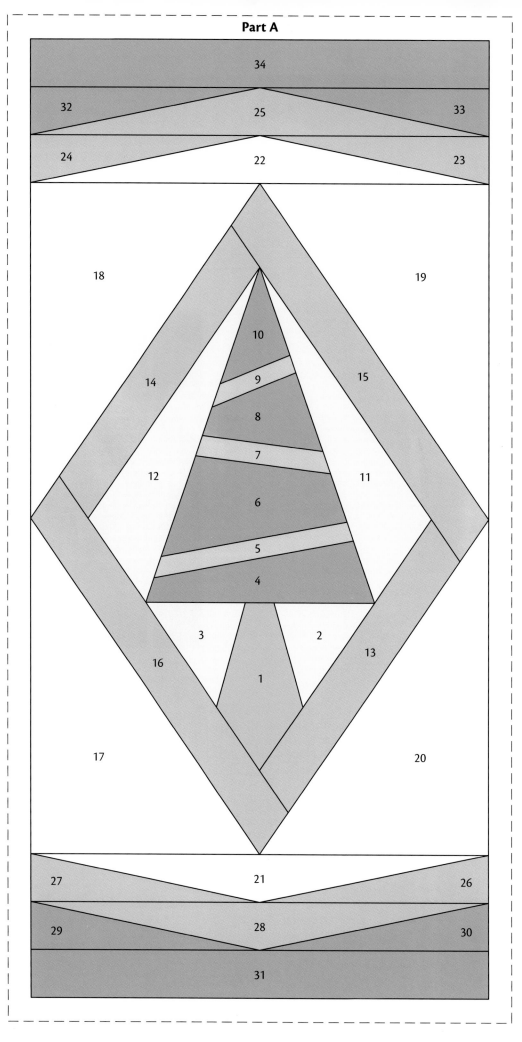

**Part A**

Make 1 copy.

**Part B**

Make 2 copies.

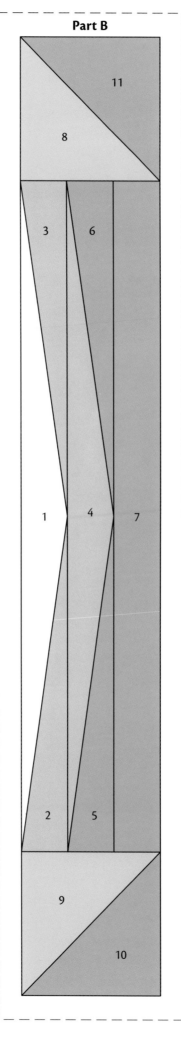

# Summer

**Finished Quilt: 9" x 9"**

*Since the striking pink stripes continue from row to row, this quilt creates the impression that it might be difficult to make. Of course, by now you know that it only appears to be so. Use your scraps for this bright little number, and check out another color scheme on page 54.*

Skill Level: Intermediate

# Materials

- 1 fat quarter of multicolored purple leaf fabric for outer border, backing, and binding
- 14" x 18" scrap of pink solid or hand-dyed fabric for patchwork strips
- 11" x 18" scrap of green solid or hand-dyed fabric for middle border, corner blocks, and patchwork strips
- 12" x 12" scrap of purple solid or hand-dyed fabric for patchwork strips
- 8" x 9" scrap of white-on-white print for inner border
- 10" x 10" piece of batting

# Cutting

**From the white-on-white print, cut:**
4 strips, 1½" x 7"

**From the green solid or hand-dyed fabric, cut:**
4 strips, 1¼" x 7"
4 squares, 2½" x 2½"

**From the multicolored purple leaf print, cut:**
4 strips, 1¾" x 7"
1 square, 10" x 10"
3 strips, 1¼" x 20"

# Assembly and Finishing

1. Copy or trace the foundation patterns on pages 54–55 onto your preferred foundation material. Make one copy each of parts A, B, and C, and two copies of part D.

2. Referring to "How to Paper Piece These Quilts" on page 6, paper piece parts A–D. Refer to the quilt diagram below and the project photo as a guide for fabric placement. As you complete the parts, assemble the quilt top as follows:
   - Join A and C to opposite sides of B.
   - Join the D parts to the top and bottom of the quilt.

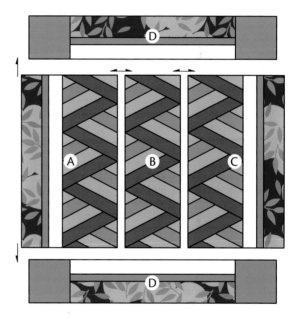

3. Referring to "Traditional Single-Fold Binding" on page 10, layer the 10" x 10" multicolored backing piece, the batting, and the quilt top; baste. Quilt as desired. Bind the quilt edges with the 1¼" x 20" multicolored strips.

*Select and stitch a colorful array of batik scraps and you will have a real eye-catcher to display in your home.*

**Part B**

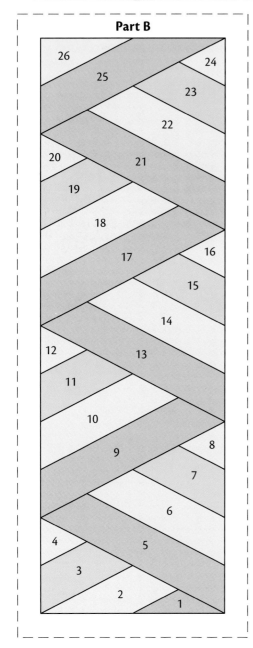

Make 1 copy.

**Part A**

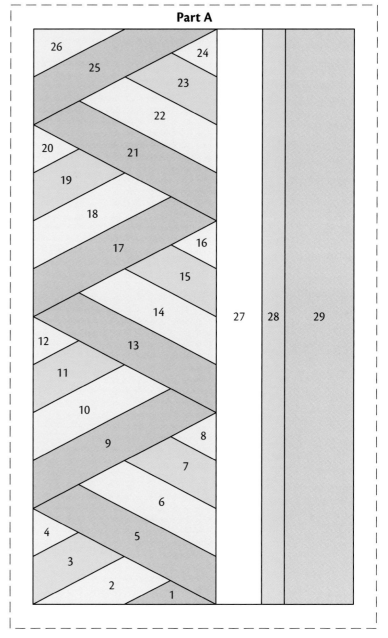

Make 1 copy.

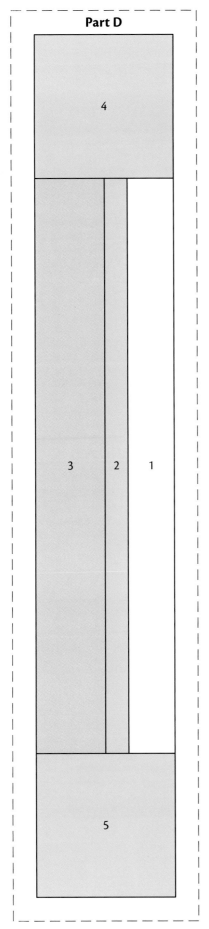

Make 2 copies.

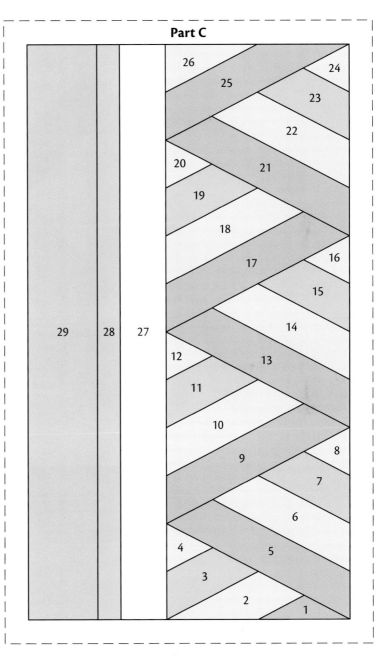

Make 1 copy.

# Early Autumn

**Finished Quilt: 9" x 11"**

*Here's another mini quilt you can make from all sorts of scraps. If you wish, you can rearrange the rows, which will give the quilt another—totally different—look. See one suggestion on page 57.*

Skill Level: Advanced

# Materials

- 1 fat quarter of brown marbled print for outer border, backing, and binding
- 18" x 22" *total* of assorted green prints for patchwork strips
- 18" x 22" *total* of assorted yellow and orange prints for patchwork strips
- 11" x 13" scrap of green leaf print for inner border and corner blocks
- 10" x 12" piece of batting

# Cutting

**From the green leaf print, cut:**
2 strips, 1½" x 9"
2 strips, 1½" x 7"
4 squares, 2½" x 2½"

**From the brown marbled print, cut:**
2 strips, 2¼" x 9"
2 strips, 2¼" x 7"
1 rectangle, 10" x 12"
3 strips, 1¼" x 20"

# Assembly and Finishing

1. Copy or trace the foundation patterns on page 58 onto your preferred foundation material. Make two copies each of parts A and C, and four copies of part B.

2. Referring to "How to Paper Piece These Quilts" on page 6, paper piece parts A–C. Refer to the quilt diagram above right and the project photo as a guide for fabric placement. As you complete the parts, assemble the quilt top as follows:
   - Join A to B (AB).
   - Rotate part B 180° and join it to AB (ABBr).
   - Join ABBr to B (ABBrB).
   - Rotate part B 180° and join it to ABBrB (ABBrBBr).
   - Join ABBrBBr to the remaining A.
   - Join the C parts to the top and bottom of the quilt.

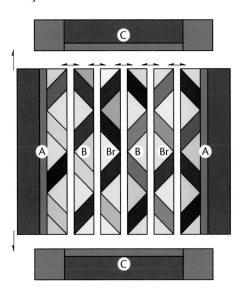

3. Referring to "Traditional Single-Fold Binding" on page 10, layer the 10" x 12" brown marbled backing piece, the batting, and the quilt top; baste. Quilt as desired. Bind the quilt edges with the 1¼" x 20" brown marbled strips.

## MINI TIP

*Try interchanging the rows (here I used A-Br-Br-B-B-A) and see what interesting variations you can come up with!*

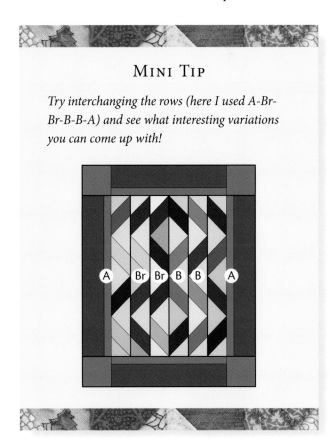

**Part C**

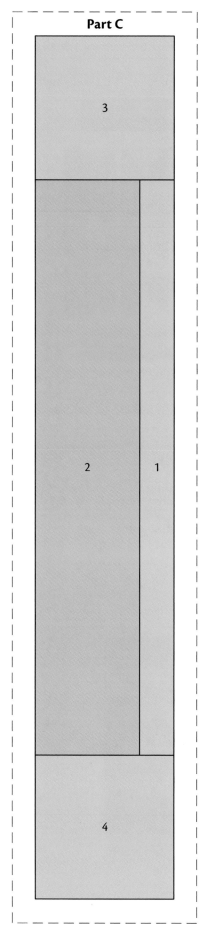

Make 2 copies.

**Part B**

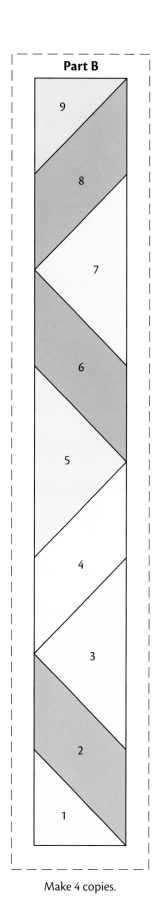

Make 4 copies.

**Part A**

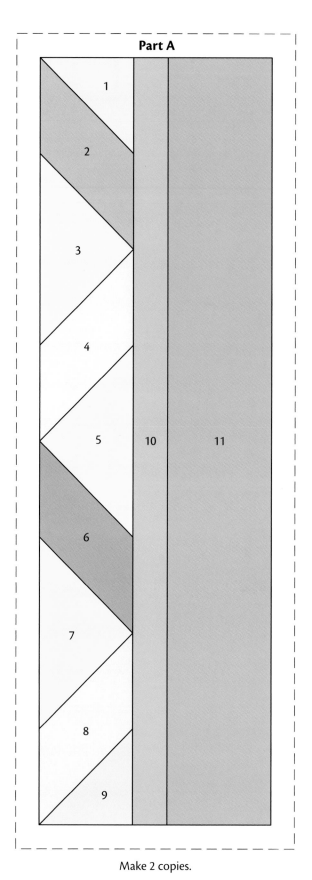

Make 2 copies.

# Geese in the Air

**Finished Quilt: 8" x 9"**

*This flying-geese quilt is made from only five parts—ideal, even for confident beginners.*

**Skill Level: Intermediate**

# Materials

- 1 fat quarter of turquoise marbled print for outer border, backing, and binding
- 12" x 17" scrap of subtle cream print for middle border and background
- 8" x 18" *total* of assorted blue print scraps for patchwork geese
- 9" x 12" scrap of dark blue print for inner border and corner blocks
- 9" x 10" piece of batting

# Cutting

**From the dark blue print, cut:**
2 strips, 1¼" x 7"
2 strips, 1¼" x 6"
4 squares, 2½" x 2½"

**From the subtle cream print, cut:**
2 strips, 1¼" x 7"
2 strips, 1¼" x 6"

**From the turquoise marbled print, cut:**
2 strips, 1¾" x 7"
2 strips, 1¾" x 6"
1 rectangle, 9" x 10"
3 strips, 1¼" x 20"

# Assembly and Finishing

1. Copy or trace the foundation patterns on pages 61–62 onto your preferred foundation material. Make one copy each of parts A, B, and C, and two copies of part D.

2. Referring to "How to Paper Piece These Quilts" on page 6, paper piece parts A–D. Refer to the quilt diagram below and the project photo on page 59 as a guide for fabric placement. As you complete the parts, assemble the quilt top as follows:
   - Join A and C to the top and bottom of B.
   - Join the D parts to the sides of the quilt.

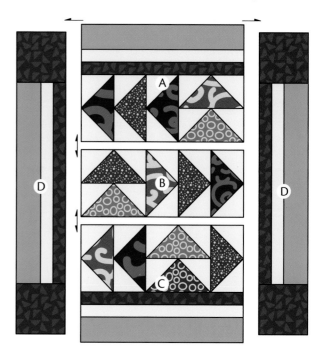

3. Referring to "Traditional Single-Fold Binding" on page 10, layer the 9" x 10" turquoise backing piece, the batting, and the quilt top; baste. Quilt as desired. Bind the quilt edges with the 1¼" x 20" turquoise strips.

*My mum made this black-and-white (with red) version of "Geese in the Air." She had wanted to make a black-and-white quilt for a long time, so now she can cross this wish off her "someday" list and start another project!*

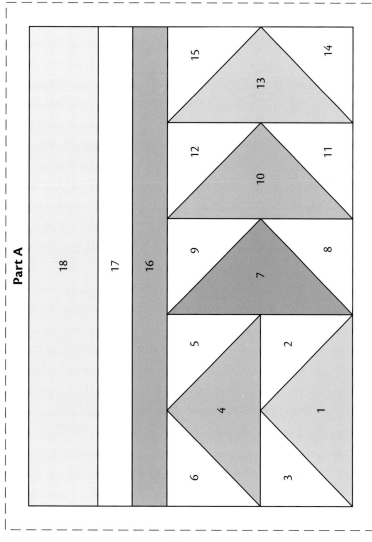

Make 1 copy.

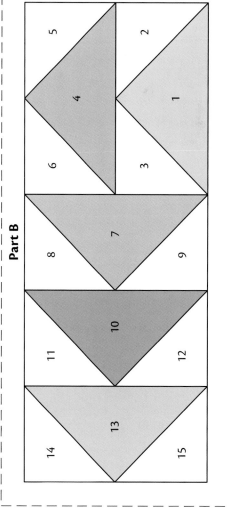

Make 1 copy.

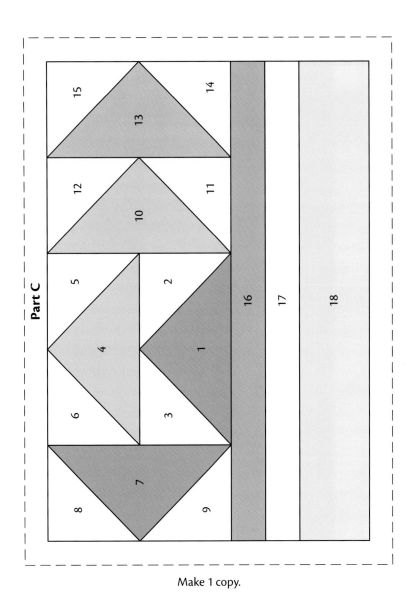

Make 1 copy.

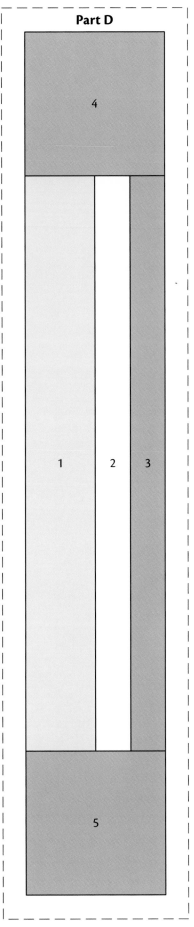

Make 2 copies.

# Plaid Quilt

**Finished Quilt: 10" x 11"**

*I* have never, ever witnessed such a dramatic change in a quilt caused by choosing different fabrics! For this version, I used a variety of plaids for a sturdy country look. Wait until you see the alternate quilt on page 65!

Skill Level: Intermediate

# Materials

- 1 fat quarter of brown plaid for outer border, patchwork strips, backing, and binding
- 18" x 22" *total* of assorted plaid scraps for patchwork strips
- 11" x 12" scrap of dark blue plaid for middle border and corner blocks
- 11" x 11" scrap of yellowish orange plaid for inner border and sashing
- 11" x 12" piece of batting

# Cutting

**From the yellowish orange plaid, cut:**
4 strips, 1½" x 9"
2 strips, 1½" x 8"

**From the dark blue plaid, cut:**
2 strips, 1¼" x 9"
2 strips, 1¼" x 8"
4 squares, 2½" x 2½"

**From the brown plaid, cut:**
2 strips, 1¾" x 9"
2 strips, 1¾" x 8"
1 rectangle, 11" x 12"
3 strips, 1¼" x 20"

# Assembly and Finishing

1. Copy or trace the foundation patterns on pages 65–67 onto your preferred foundation material. Make one copy each of parts A, B, and C, and two copies of part D.

2. Referring to "How to Paper Piece These Quilts" on page 6, paper piece parts A–D. Refer to the quilt diagram below and the project photo on page 63 as a guide for fabric placement. As you complete the parts, assemble the quilt top as follows:
   - Join A and C to opposite sides of B.
   - Join the D parts to the top and bottom of the quilt.

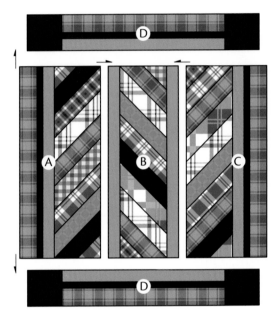

3. Referring to "Traditional Single-Fold Binding" on page 10, layer the 11" x 12" brown plaid backing piece, the batting, and the quilt top; baste. Quilt as desired. Bind the quilt edges with the 1¼" x 20" brown plaid strips.

*Do you believe it? Here is the same design, but this time with very dainty floral prints . . . and you have a lovely quilt for spring!*

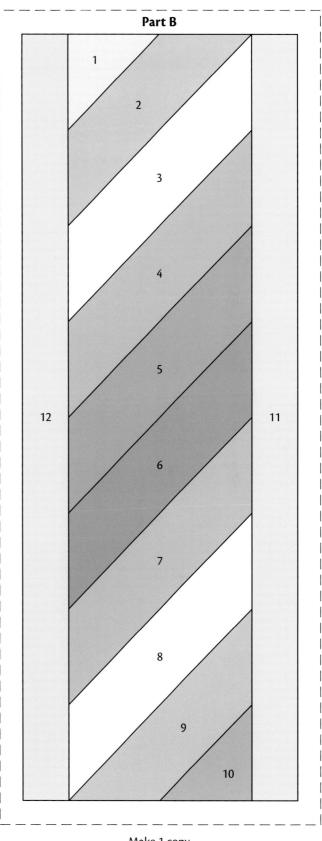

**Part B**

1
2
3
4
5
6
7
8
9
10
11
12

Make 1 copy.

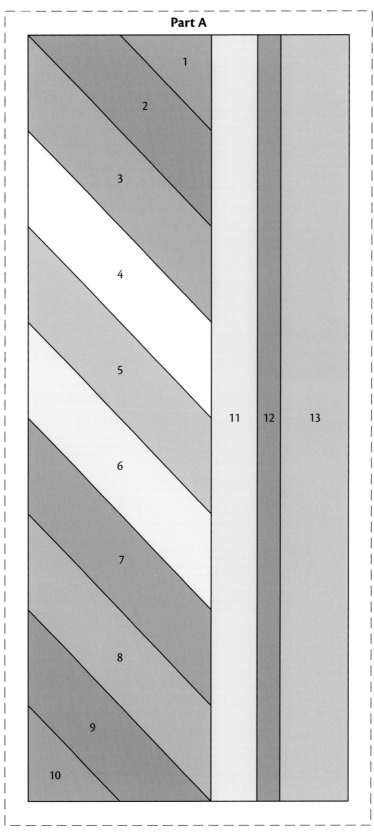

Make 1 copy.

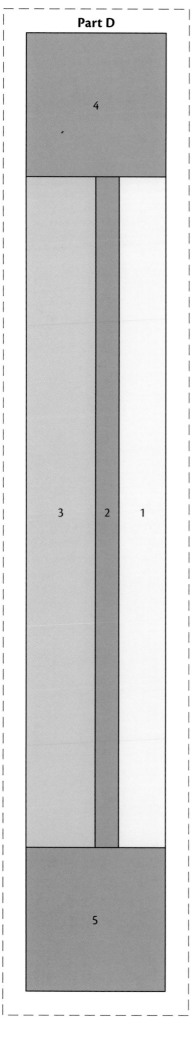

**Part D**

4

Make 2 copies.

3    2    1

5

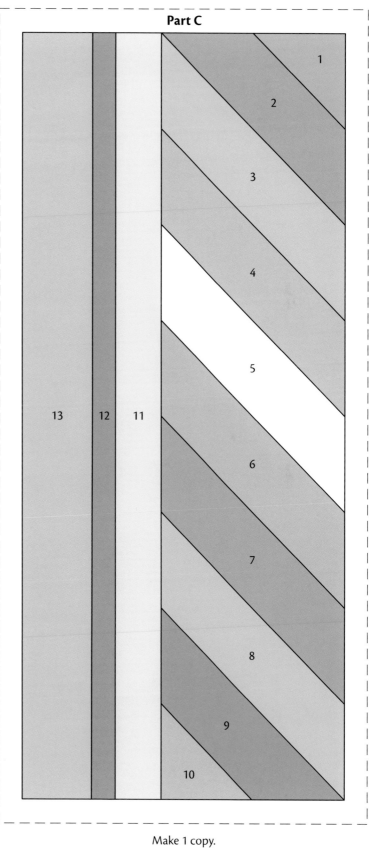

**Part C**

1

2

3

4

5

6

7

8

9

10

13    12    11

Make 1 copy.

# Indian Summer

**Finished Quilt: 9½" x 12"**

*The autumn-like quilt shown here is just one of the many looks you can create with these charming pinwheels. Imagine a Christmas quilt made with red and green pinwheels; red, white, and blue pinwheels for the Fourth of July; or a variety of lovely pastel pinwheels to celebrate spring. Let your creativity run away with you.*

Skill Level: Intermediate

# Materials

- 22" x 22" piece of brown-and-black leaf print for outer border, backing, and binding
- 1 fat quarter of cream print for background, sashing, and inner border
- 9" x 18" scrap of green print for pinwheels and corner blocks
- 9" x 12" scrap of yellow print for pinwheels
- 9" x 12" scrap of dark brown marbled print for pinwheels
- 9" x 12" scrap of reddish brown print for pinwheels
- 10½" x 13" piece of batting

# Cutting

**From the cream print, cut:**
2 strips, 2½" x 10"
2 strips, 2½" x 7½"
1 strip, 1½" x 10"

**From the brown-and-black leaf print, cut:**
4 strips, 2½" x 5½"
4 strips, 2½" x 4¼"
1 rectangle, 10½" x 13"
3 strips, 1¼" x 20"

**From the green print, cut:**
4 squares, 2½" x 2½"

# Assembly and Finishing

1. Copy or trace the foundation patterns on pages 70–72 onto your preferred foundation material. Make one copy each of parts A, B, C, and D, and two copies of part E.

2. Referring to "How to Paper Piece These Quilts" on page 6, paper piece parts A–E. Refer to the quilt diagram below and the project photo as a guide for fabric placement. As you complete the parts, assemble the quilt top as follows:
   - Join A to B (AB).
   - Join AB to C (ABC).
   - Join ABC to D.
   - Join the E parts to the top and bottom of the quilt.

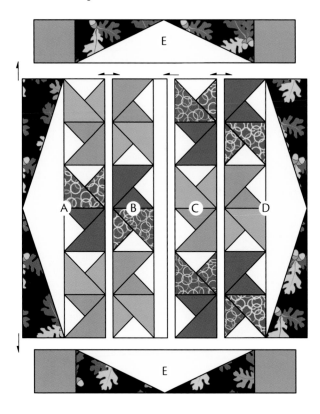

3. Referring to "Traditional Single-Fold Binding" on page 10, layer the 10½" x 13" leaf print backing piece, the batting, and the quilt top; baste. Quilt as desired. Bind the quilt edges with the 1¼" x 20" leaf print strips.

**Part B**

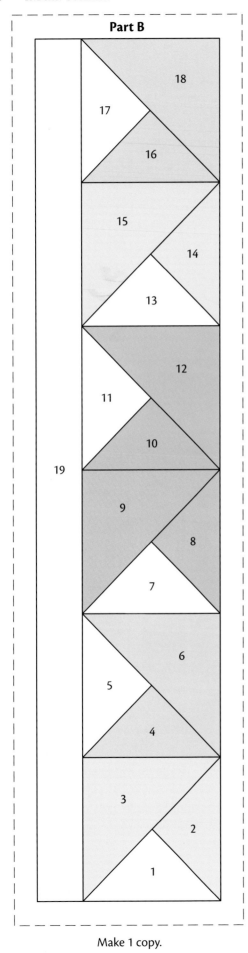

Make 1 copy.

**Part A**

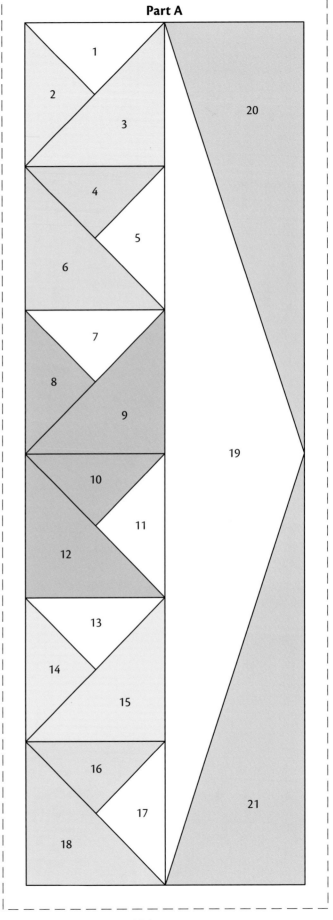

Make 1 copy.

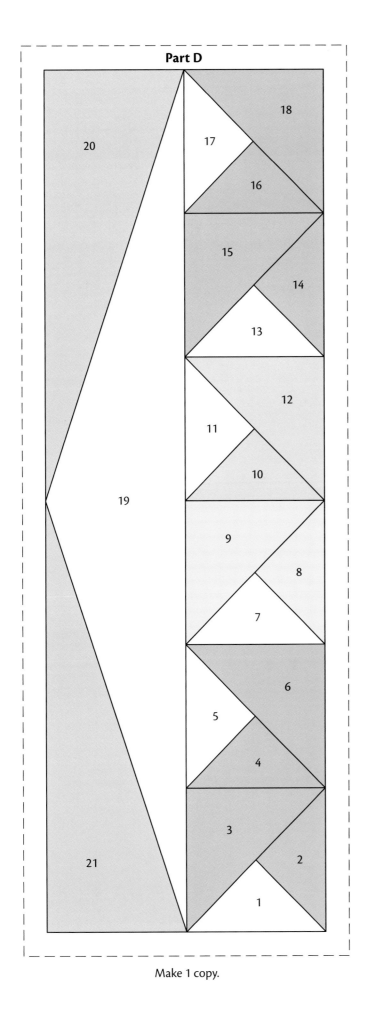

**Part D**

Make 1 copy.

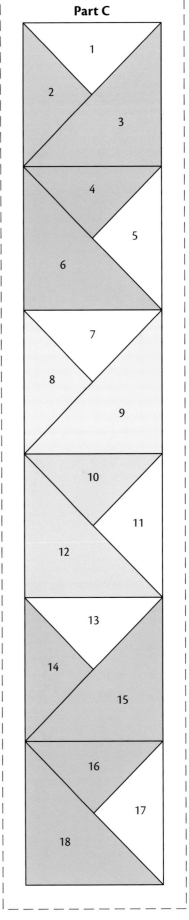

**Part C**

Make 1 copy.

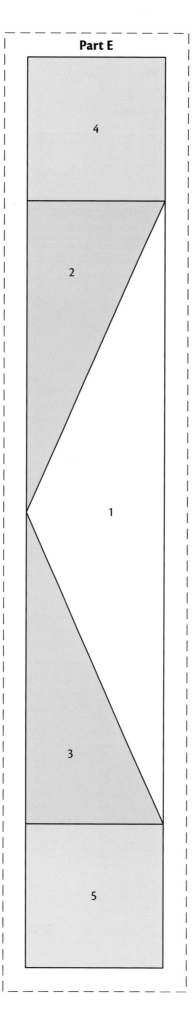

**Part E**

Make 2 copies.

# Farmland

**Finished Quilt: 7" x 9"**

*This sweet little farm quilt requires only one part—even an absolute newbie to patchwork will achieve charming results.*

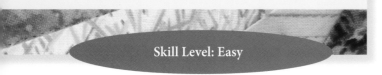

Skill Level: Easy

# Materials

- 15" x 20" scrap of corn print for outer border, backing, and optional binding
- 18" x 18" *total* of assorted print scraps for fields
- 7" x 10" scrap of black solid fabric for inner border
- 7" x 9" scrap of blue print for sky
- Assorted small scraps for farm, roof, and silo
- 7" x 9" piece of batting

# Cutting

**From the blue print, cut:**
1 strip, 2" x 4½"
1 strip, 2" x 6"

**From the black solid fabric, cut:**
2 strips, 1¼" x 8"
2 strips, 1¼" x 6½"

**From the corn print, cut:**
2 strips, 1¾" x 8½"
2 strips, 1¾" x 8"
1 rectangle, 8" x 10"
2 strips, 1¼" x 20" (for optional binding)

# Assembly and Finishing

The quilt shown on page 73 is finished using the birthing method described on page 9. If you prefer a binding, refer to "Traditional Single-Fold Binding" on page 10. For that method, use an 8" x 10" piece of batting, prepare the quilt for quilting as instructed, and use the 1¼" x 20" corn print strips to bind the quilt edges.

1.  Copy or trace the foundation pattern on page 75 onto your preferred foundation material. Make one copy.

2.  Referring to "How to Paper Piece These Quilts" on page 6, paper piece the foundation. Refer to the quilt diagram below and the project photo on page 73 as a guide for fabric placement.

3.  Referring to "The Birthing Method" on page 9, prepare the quilt sandwich (quilt top, batting, and 8" x 10" corn print backing piece) for quilting. Quilt as desired.

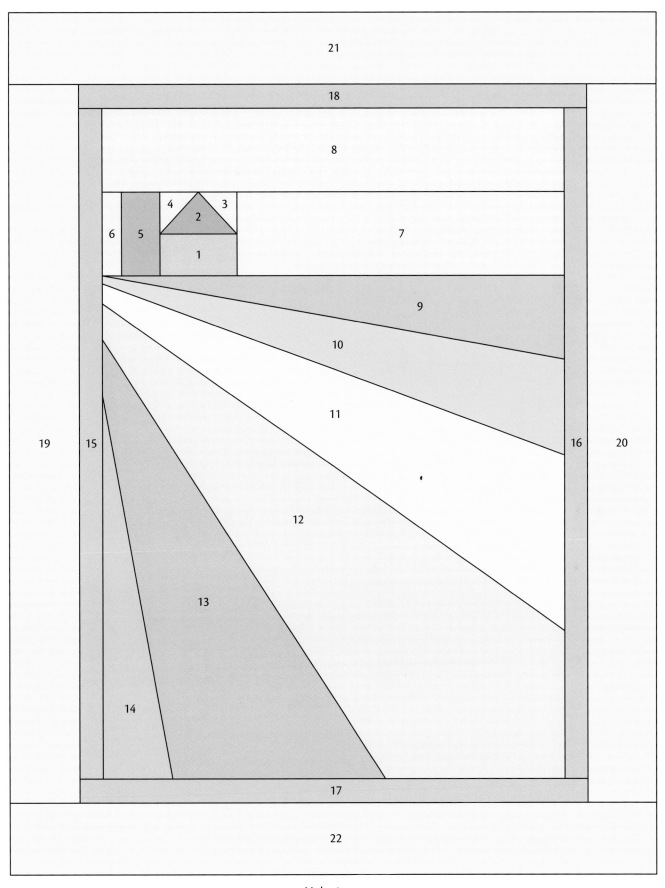

Make 1 copy.

# Sunshine Quilt

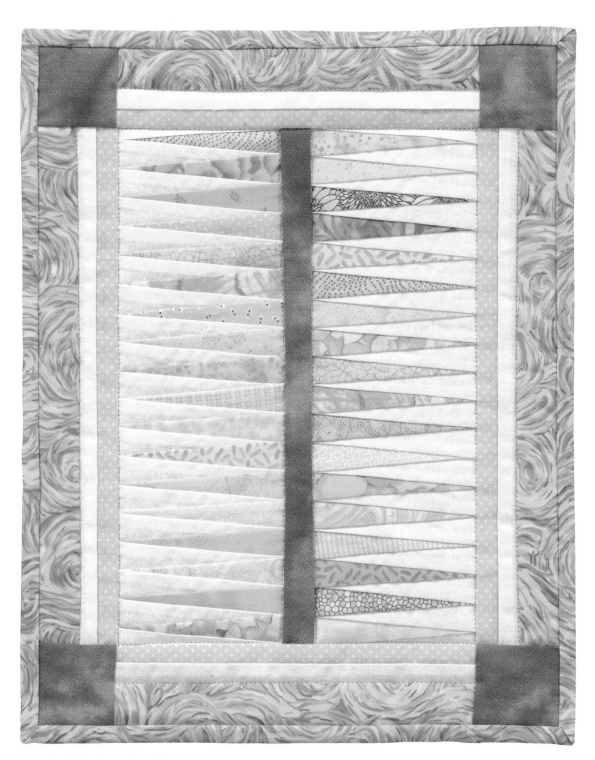

**Finished Quilt: 9½" x 12"**

*This mini quilt brings the sun into your home and looks terrific against a dark wall. Although the project consists of only four parts, I have given it an advanced skill rating, as you must work very carefully to achieve sharp, accurate points.*

Skill Level: Advanced

# Materials

- 22" x 22" piece of white-on-white print for middle border and background
- 22" x 22" piece of dark yellow-and-orange print for outer border, backing, and binding
- 18" x 22" *total* of assorted yellow, orange, and yellow-and-orange print scraps for patchwork points
- 10" x 12" scrap of orange marbled or hand-dyed fabric for corner blocks and sashing
- 7" x 12" scrap of light yellow print for inner border
- 10½" x 13" piece of batting

# Cutting

**From the white-on-white print, cut:**
2 strips, 1¼" x 10"
2 strips, 1¼" x 7½"

**From the light yellow print, cut:**
2 strips, 1¼" x 10"
2 strips, 1¼" x 7½"

**From the dark yellow-and-orange print, cut:**
2 strips, 1¾" x 10"
2 strips, 1¾" x 7½"
1 rectangle, 10½" x 13"
3 strips, 1¼" x 20"

**From the orange marbled or hand-dyed fabric, cut:**
1 strip, 1½" x 10"
4 squares, 2½" x 2½"

# Assembly and Finishing

1. Copy or trace the foundation patterns on pages 78–80 onto your preferred foundation material. Make one copy each of parts A and B, and two copies of part C.

2. Referring to "How to Paper Piece These Quilts" on page 6, paper piece parts A–C. Refer to the quilt diagram below and the project photo as a guide for fabric placement. As you complete the parts, assemble the quilt top as follows:
   - Join A to B.
   - Join the C parts to the top and bottom of the quilt.

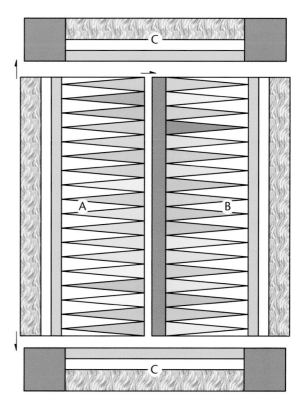

3. Referring to "Traditional Single-Fold Binding" on page 10, layer the 10½" x 13" yellow-and-orange print backing piece, the batting, and the quilt top; baste. Quilt as desired. Bind the quilt edges with the 1¼" x 20" yellow-and-orange print strips.

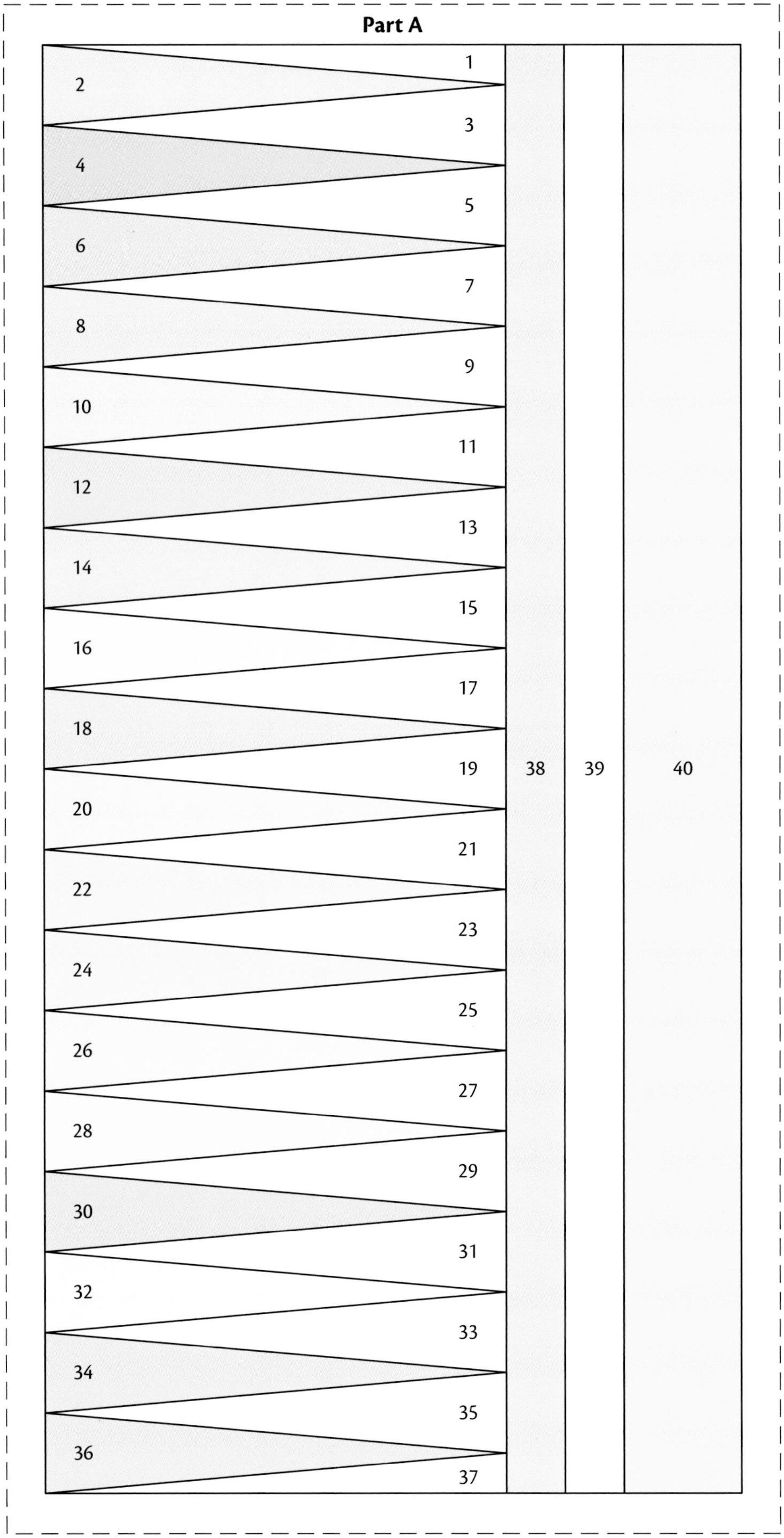

**Part A**

| 1 |
|---|
| 2 |
| 3 |
| 4 |
| 5 |
| 6 |
| 7 |
| 8 |
| 9 |
| 10 |
| 11 |
| 12 |
| 13 |
| 14 |
| 15 |
| 16 |
| 17 |
| 18 |
| 19 |
| 20 |
| 21 |
| 22 |
| 23 |
| 24 |
| 25 |
| 26 |
| 27 |
| 28 |
| 29 |
| 30 |
| 31 |
| 32 |
| 33 |
| 34 |
| 35 |
| 36 |
| 37 |

38   39   40

Make 1 copy.

**Part B**

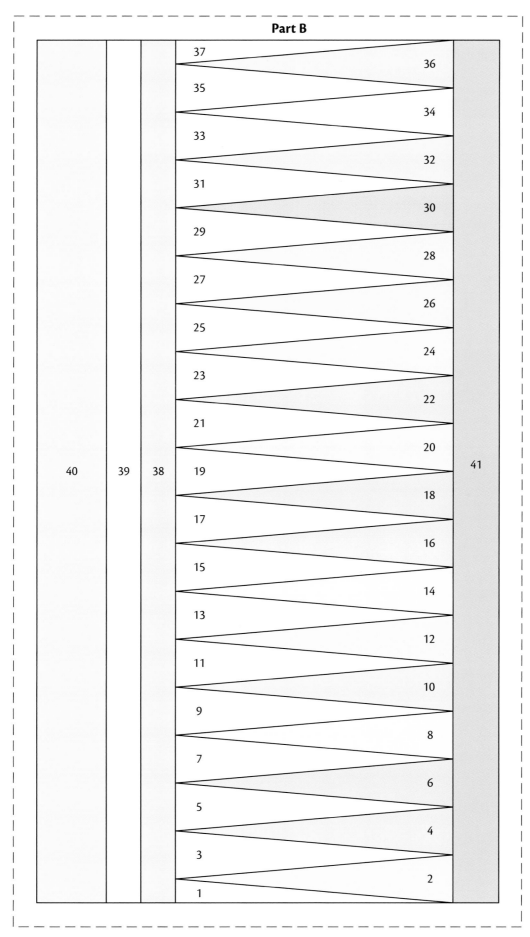

Make 1 copy.

**Part C**

4

3    2    1

5

**Part C**

Make 2 copies.

# About the Author

WENDY VOSTERS WAS attracted to crafts at an early age, learning how to knit, embroider, crochet, and even make dolls. Her mum—who never, ever sits still—set the example. Wendy got her first sewing machine at age 13 and started to make her own clothes. No, not the ordinary clothes you saw everywhere, but garments embellished with cross-stitch, ribbons, and appliqués! She even made a very fine cutwork blouse for her granny, who always wore it with pride.

Wendy finished high school, but also kept up with the crafts she loved so much. Even while attending conservatory (yes, she is a lecturing musician), she found time to make her own wardrobe and do a lot of embroidery as well.

In 1995, while attending a quilt show, Wendy became fascinated by the beautiful quilts on display. A new hobby was born—patchwork! She took a basic course in quiltmaking, and since then she has never stopped quilting. Nowadays, she designs patterns for various patchwork shops in the Netherlands. Most of the patterns are for paper piecing—her favorite technique.

Wendy is happily married to Piet van den Eeden and lives with him, her mum, and four dogs in a town in the southern part of the Netherlands. Fortunately her mum is a very enthusiastic quilter as well, so they are never short of topics of conversation. Wendy's husband is often out on the sea fishing in his spare time, which leaves Wendy plenty of opportunity to enjoy her favorite pastime—quilting! Visit Wendy's Web site at www.wendyvosters.com.